SCOTLAND'S BARD

A concise biography of Robert Burns
(1759 - 1796)

by Norman R Paton

Sea-Green Ribbon Publications

By The Same Author

THE JACOBITES - Their Roots, Rebellions and Links with Freemasonry.
SONG O' LIBERTY - The Politics of Robert Burns
THOU LINGERING STAR - The Legend of Highland Mary

COPYRIGHT NORRIE PATON 1998
ISBN 0 9522944 4 3

Published by: Sea-Green Ribbon Publications
Fareham, Hampshire

Printed in England by: Consort Print Services, Consort Court, Fareham.

As Burns Saw It

Gie me ae spark o' Nature's fire,
That's a' the learning I desire;
Then tho' I drudge thro' dub an' mire
    At pleugh or cart,
My Muse, tho' hamely in attire,
    May touch the heart

Epistle to John Lapraik.

For me! before a Monarch's face,
    Ev'n *there* I winna flatter;
For neither Pension, Post, nor Place,
    Am I your humble debtor:

A Dream.

O wad some Pow'r the giftie gie us
To see oursels as others see us!

To a Louse.

Tho' now they ca' me, Fornicator,
And tease my name in kintra clatter,
The mair they talk, I'm kend the better;
    E'en let them clash!
An auld wife's tongue's a feckless matter
    To gie ane fash.-

Welcome to a Bastart Wean.

This warld's wealth when I think on,
    Its pride, and a' the lave o't;
My curse on silly coward man,
    That he should be the slave o't

O Poortith Cauld.

Then gently scan your brother Man,
    Still gentler sister Woman;
Tho' they may gang a kennin wrang,
    To step aside is human:

Address to the Unco Guid.

BURNS was a poor man, from birth; & an Exciseman, by necessity: but - I will say it! - the sterling of his honest worth, no poverty could debase; & his independent British mind, Oppression might bend, but could not subdue.-

Letter to John Erskine of Mar.

God knows I am no Saint; I have a whole host of Follies & Sins to answer for; but if I could, & I believe I do it as far as I can, I would wipe away all tears from all eyes.

Letter to Peter Hill.

O what insignificant sordid wretches are they, however chance may have loaded them with wealth, who go to their graves, to their magnificent mausoleums, with hardly the consciousness of having made one poor honest heart happy.

Letter to Maria Riddell.

CONTENTS

LIST OF PLATES

FRONT COVER:
Chalk drawing of Robert Burns by Archibald Skirving. The quotation is from the poem: *To the Guidwife of Wauchope House.*

BACK COVER:
The poet's seal, which he described in a letter to Alexander Cunningham, 3 March, 1794. The quotation, by Catherine Carswell, is taken from her *Life of Robert Burns* (reprinted 1990) p. 400.

Introduction

The story of Robert Burns might well be woven around the theme of wine, women and song if his reputation, among some sections of his ain folk, was anything to go by. There was certainly much greater substance to Burns, however, than the popular, but misleading legend, of a gifted ploughman who could write heaven-inspired poetry, but spent too much of his precious spare time in drinking bouts, or chasing after women whom he immortalized in song. It is of considerable importance to know that Burns was a democrat at a time when those around him weren't quite sure what democracy was, whilst those in power, who were well aware of what it meant, took repressive measures to prevent its progress. Burns also shook the Kirk of Scotland and the fundamental tenets of Calvinism with a series of devastating satires; he was, however, proud to count among his friends, priests, both Catholic and Protestant, who served the people with a religious comfort by rejecting the doctrine of hell-fire and damnation. He had sympathies of the sentimental kind for the fallen House of Stuart and the Jacobites who perished in their cause, but at heart he was essentially a bard of the people, and it must not be overlooked that he risked much to voice their wrongs. Yet, the popular concept of a poet who glorified in wine, women and song remains a useful means of presenting introductory remarks.

As a poet, Burns was a first rate literary craftsman - as a songwriter he was something else. The *Concise Cambridge History of English Literature* has claimed that, any fifty of his songs would have to be named in a compiled list of the world's best songs. It is surely an exaggeration; yet, to claim that his finest fifty songs - what a task to select them - must be included in the best of the world's songs, takes us onto more secure ground, and defies contradiction. Burns the songwriter, by whatever standards, is recognized in the international field as an artist supreme! It is difficult to believe that he was not a singer, and the possibility remains that the comments made by his schoolmaster have rather distorted the truth; he was, after all, a mere six year old bairn, when John Murdoch formed the opinion for posterity that Robert Burns was tone deaf.

It is certainly true that very few of his contemporaries laid claim to

i

hearing him sing. Jane Jaffray, *The Blue-eyed Lassie,* did recall him singing to her, but only in a rather casual manner. He had frequently visited her parents' home, and she vividly remembered the occasion, in her sixteenth year, when Burns had hoisted her high into the air, and, as he danced and capered around, sang *Green Grow the Rashes,* before placing her in her father's carriage. Jane chose to live in America after her subsequent marriage, and she socialized with some famous people there, including Washington Irving, but none ever eclipsed the big, genial exciseman of her Scottish adolescence. She appreciated her song, *The Blue-eyed Lassie,* but preferred the other one he had written for her, *When First I Saw,* though some editors, including James Kinsley, have rejected it as spurious.

There were numerous women in Burns's short life, and most of them ended up as the heroine of one song or another. Some, alas, such as Bess Paton, May Cameron, Jenny Clow, and Ann Park were little more than sexual fodder, though Ms Park, whose daughter to him was accepted into his family, sparked his Muse into the fine song, *The Gowden Locks of Anna.* His first serious affair was with a young housekeeper employed in a mansion by Cessnock Water; she was long known by the name Ellison Begbie, until James Mackay's exceptional biography established her real identity as Elizabeth Gebbie. Burns had hoped to marry her, but it was not to be, and her "peremptory refusal" to his proposal left him thoroughly devastated.

In the opening weeks of 1786 Burns married Jean Armour by an act of written declaration; her father disapproved when the news could no longer be withheld from him, and the marriage was declared to be over. The legalities of this matter have been much disputed; the Kirk, however, then a powerful voice in the land, informed Burns that he was a bachelor, and he acted accordingly. He looked for another wife, who might join him in a proposed emigration to Jamaica, and thought that Mary Campbell, would be suited to this role. Her tragic death in October, 1786, opened the way for his union to Jean Armour to be reinstated, but not before he had courted Peggy Chalmers, only to be rejected when she chose a rival suitor.

On the rebound came his famous affair with Mrs Agnes McLehose. The harsh realities of James McLehose in the faraway West Indies, and Jean Armour in not so faraway Mauchline, ensured that Clarinda and Sylvander

- as they styled themselves - were acting out an epistolary fantasy. In the end Burns pledged himself to Armour, whilst Clarinda fumed at her Sylvander's "perfidious treachery".

The drinking habits of Robert Burns will provoke controversy whenever, and wherever, his very name is spoken. The concept of Burns as a degenerate drunkard, and hopeless alcoholic, is as repugnant as it is false. The pendulum, however, has also been allowed to swing too far the other way - Robin and John Barleycorn were certainly more than mere nodding acquaintances. The bard who wished that Parnassus had been a vineyard, was merely playing for effect, but he did enjoy his fair share of port wine! His wife said that he drank rum and brandy at home - this is hardly surprising, as his Excise "perks" brought him a plentiful supply of both. Whisky, however, was the drink of the day, and his cronies would have insisted that, if he could sing its praises in verse, he could down it in their company. He gave to each of them, "a slice of his constitution", and he gave it willingly enough. Those who latched onto the phrase, and wished that he had given much thinner slices, simply lamented in vain. It was too late to matter!

It is inconceivable that Burns would have demurely declined to have his glass topped up when in the bosom of good company. Ensconced in a comfortable howff, fast by an ingle blazing finely, with the drink in full flow, the talk and wit of Burns would have been utterly glorious! Care, mad to see a man sae happy! - and damn the one who would draw his attention to the time, and remind him that his Excise tasks awaited him come the dawn. Those who deny this image of Burns, deny him his hail and hearty fellowship, and larger-than-life personality. They attempt to invent a mere stuffed shirt, by suppressing a social colossus.

The real Robert Burns has probably gone for ever, lost in a labyrinth of well intentioned legends, packaged by doting admirers, and sometimes surly enemies, into a socially convenient slot of their own created concept. Ian McIntyre (1995) made a very creditable attempt to present a life of Burns based on known facts; like Snyder in 1932, he was cautious about venturing too deeply into the legend. James Mackay, on the other hand, in his lengthy 1992 biography, has delved liberally and deeply, and sprinkled his book with many controversial opinions. I do not agree with him on several issues, but I did find his book extremely useful and thoroughly entertaining. My own preferred book on the poet is Thomas Crawford's outstanding, *Burns: A Study of the Poems and Songs.* I can now only hope that, the story which unfolds in the ensuing pages, brings a measure of interest to those who enjoy reading about the remarkable character named Robert Burns.

***

The quotations given from the poems and songs are based on the text of the Oxford University Clarendon Press edition of Burns, edited by James Kinsley, 1968, with the poem number referenced in the source notes. Where the first line of a poem is not given in the quotation, it follows the poem number in the notes, to allow the poem, or song, to be readily identified in any alternative edition. The quotations from Burns's letters are based on the two-volume edition, Clarendon Press, Oxford, 1931, edited by, John De Lancey Ferguson, 2nd edition ed. G Ross Roy, 1985. In all cases, Burns's own spelling of words which may be suspect of error, has been retained, without comment to this effect, in the accompanying text.

CHAPTER ONE

No Distant Pretensions

I have not the most distant pretensions to what the pyecoated
guardians of escutcheons call, A Gentleman. - When at
Edinburgh last winter, I got acquainted in the Herald's Office,
and looking through that granary of Honors I there found almost
every name in the kingdom; but for me,
     "-My ancient but ignoble blood
Has crept thro' Scoundrels ever since the flood."

                                        Robert Burns
                                        Autobiography

It was the year 1748 that William Burnes, son of a poverty stricken farmer in the north-east of Scotland, decided that his future lay in bidding farewell to his native heath, and setting forth for what he deemed the more prosperous pastures of the lowlands. His eldest brother James chose to settle in Montrose, but William, in the company of another brother, Robert, two years older than himself, had the capital city of Edinburgh in mind. They had meandered down past the Howe of the Mearns, through the city of Perth, across the River Tay and after the anguish of parting when Robert decided to continue his journey south, over the border into England, William took his separate path to Edinburgh.

He had reasoned that gardening work might provide the best means of employment and was soon engaged landscaping the great park now known as the Meadows, which lies to the south of the Royal Infirmary. He remained in this work for a period of two years, then decided to move across to the west coast, eventually settling in Dundonald parish, where he served as gardener to a local laird, Alexander Fairlie. Again the duration of employment lasted two years before the urge to move crossed his mind once more. By 1754 William Burnes had settled close to the hamlet of Alloway, and shortly afterwards he accepted the position of head gardener to the Provost of Ayr, Dr William Fergusson, who had recently returned to the area after a medical career in London.

In the summer of 1756 William Burnes's life took another twist when he met a girl at Maybole Fair who was to bring his bachelor status to an end at the age of thirty-five: her name was Agnes Brown, and she was eleven years younger than the husband she married on the 15 December 1757. In preparation of his betrothal William Burnes had obtained ground at Alloway and had erected a small cottage on it by his own labours: it was completed and ready to house them immediately after their wedding.

The cottage was the birthplace (but only just) of their first born child, a boy. His arrival was dated the 25 January 1759, and within a few days the raging winter storms had created structural damage of such extent to their home that it forced mother and son to be escorted to the sheltering safety of a nearby farmhouse.

> Our monarch's hindmost year but ane   (one)
> Was five-and-twenty days begun,
> 'Twas then a blast o' Janwar' Win'   (January Wind)
> Blew hansel in on Robin.[1]   (heralded Robin's birth)

On the following day, William Burnes rode into Ayr and sought the services of the Revd. William Dalrymple for the purposes of baptizing the infant. Dalrymple duly agreed to accompany William back to the cottage as soon as the official birth entry had been registered by the clerk, who, on being informed of the family name, obviously assumed it to follow the Ayrshire spelling, and copied into his ledger the following entry:

> Robert Burns, lawful son to William Burns, in Alloway, and Agnes Brown, his spouse, was born January 25, 1759; bapd. 26, by Mr William Dalrymple. Witnesses: John Tennant and Jas. Young.

No biographical details of James Young have survived - the other witness, John Tennant, has long been regarded as a local farmer who remained a lifelong friend of the Burnes's, with the ties binding the two families continuing in the years after William's death. There was, however, another John Tennant, a blacksmith at Alloway, and cousin of the farmer, who happened to be married to the local midwife, making it a distinct possibility that he had been the witness at the registration of the Burnes birth.

In the following year Agnes gave birth to a second son; he was named Gilbert after his maternal grandfather. In all, the Burneses had seven children; Robert and Gilbert being followed by Agnes (1762); Annabella (1764); William (1767); John (1769), the family being completed with daughter Isobel, born 27 June 1771. John Burns died in 1785, and lies buried in Mauchline churchyard; William died in London, where he was employed as a saddler, on 24 July 1790 - the other members of the family all survived their famous elder brother. His mother outlived him by twenty-four years, though his father, after suffering ill-health for some time, died in the early part of 1784, at the age of sixty-three.

The name Burnes or Burness has been regarded as a corruption of Burnhouse, which gave speculation to the possibility of family origins in the Argyll hamlet of that name, now known as Taynuilt, from the Gaelic, *Tigh an uillt,* "house by the burn". Walter Campbell of Burnhouse has been named as the forebear of the poet who, in the middle of the 17th century, decided to leave his native heath eventually settling in Kincardineshire. The name change from Campbell to Burnhouse, later Burnes, and his journey of some distance to his new home, has suggested that suspicious circumstances prompted Walter's sudden decision; his reasons, however, are now but the guesswork of the fanciful legend. James Mackay, in his much acclaimed biography of the poet, has noted:

> The prevelance of various two-syllable versions, such as Burness and Burnase, lends credibility to the Burnhouse origin, but there were many burnside homesteads in the north-east of Scotland whose names alluded to the fact, so a Burnhouse origin could just as easily have come from this area as anywhere else.....
> All that can be said with any certainty is that Robert Burns could trace his ancestry back as far as his great-great-grandfather, Walter. While it is obvious that people called Burns lived in the Mearns for centuries, the legend of the Campbells of Burnhouse cannot be entirely dismissed.[2]

In fact, on the authority of Jervise's *Memorials of Angus and the Mearns,* it is learned that the Inchbreck lands were held by people of the name Burnes as far back as 1547, perhaps a good deal longer, since this was the earliest known record, and that their descendants long continued the occupation.

On several occasions Robert Burns intimated, with no little pride, that

3

his grandfather, and namesake, had taken part in the Jacobite Rebellion of 1715. This information was presumably obtained from William Burnes, who would surely have been aware of his own father's allegiance and activities regarding the uprising, from the family stories that would have been discussed concerning the event. No specific evidence supported the poet's claim, and it has frequently been dismissed as his mock heroic boasts; however, it must be remembered that his grandfather farmed in the lands of George Keith, the Earl Marischal, a prominent Jacobite in the 1715 uprising, who later organized and led the lesser rebellion of 1719. Aristocrats such as Marischal made it their business to bring as many of their tenants into the field as they could conscript, and it is perfectly feasible that members of the Burnes family fought in the ranks of the rebels, regardless of whether or not their personal allegiance lay towards the cause.

There can be no doubt that if Robert's grandfather had played an active role in the rebellion William Burnes would have passed this information on to his own family in the strictest confidence. Ayrshire was solidly Whig, as the Earl of Kilmarnock duly discovered when he committed himself to the Jacobite cause in the 1745 campaign, and the cautious Burnes would surely have instructed Robert and Gilbert that Jacobite sympathies would ensure trouble within the Carrick and Kyle region. Gilbert, like his father, was little drawn on the subject; the impetuous poet, however, simply found it impossible not to trumpet his forebears' alleged deeds of valour with the rebels:

> Though my Fathers had not illustrious Honors and vast Properties to hazard in the contest; though they left their humble cottages only to add so many units more to the unnoted croud that followed their Leaders; yet, what they could they did, and what they had they lost: with unshaken firmness and unconcealed Political Attachments, they shook hands with Ruin for what they esteemed the cause of their King and their Country.[3]

In fact, Burns's first major biographer, James Currie, had been informed by a confidant of the family that: "a report did prevail, that (the poet's own father) had taken the field with the young chevalier" - William Burnes, had however, been prudent enough to obtain parish certificates clearing him of any involvement with the 1745 adventure of Charles

Edward Stuart. Nevertheless, Gilbert Burns persuaded Currie to suppress the reference made by Robert, in his autobiography, that his "Fathers rented land of the noble Keiths of Marshal, (sic) and had the honor to share their fate." Gilbert was obviously concerned that, in Whig Ayrshire, Jacobitism was still regarded with opprobrium; however, several other copies of the autobiography had been issued and the story was, as they say, out!

On his mother's side the poet's pedigree traced a lineage to almost the directly opposite geographical position, towards the south-west of Scotland, and of John Broun who farmed at Craigenton, Kirkoswald, at the end of the 17th century. Agnes Brown was the eldest of a family of six born to Gilbert Broun (or Brown) and Agnes Rennie, at Whitestone Cottage near Culzean. Shortly after her birth the family moved to the parish of Kirkoswald where her grandfather was then tenant at Craigenton Farm. She was barely ten years old when her mother died in May, 1742. Her father married again, but Agnes did not remain long at home, and left to reside with her maternal grandmother at Maybole. Attempts have been made to tie-in the Browns of Craigenton with the family of the Covenanter martyr John Brown, shot by the zealous Claverhouse (later Viscount Dundee), in May, 1685.[4] Brown, however, is such a common surname that scepticism must cloud the ultimate truth of this as fact, pending further specific evidence.

Doubtless the Browns of Craigenton were themselves of good Covenanting stock, as the district was renowned for its support of this cause. Indeed, Burns himself told John Ramsay of Ochtertyre that his maternal great-grandfather, the aforementioned John Broun of Craigenton, had been wounded in the skirmish at Aird's (or Ayr's) Moss, 22 July, 1680, when a troop of dragoons attacked a small band of Covenanters, led by Richard Cameron, rapidly cutting down their twenty horsemen.[5] Cameron himself was killed, and another leading figure, David Hackston of Rathillet, was captured and later executed at Edinburgh. The majority of the foot soldiers, however, managed to escape across the moor, by way of the Moss, where the dragoons were unable to follow.

Franklyn Bliss Snyder, in his biography of Burns in 1932, states that Agnes Brown's maternal grandmother had also known the persecution of "the killing times' when Claverhouse's Dragoons had swept through

Ayrshire, and down into Galloway on their determined mission to put an end to the practises of outdoor services - 'conventicles', as they were termed - being held by Presbyterian dissenters in these regions. Snyder, alas, gave no source reference or further note for this bare statement. Robert Chambers, commenting on the ancestry of the poet, emphatically declared that: "Burns believed he had both Jacobite and Covenanting blood in his veins."

THE Solemn League and Covenant
Now brings a smile, now brings a tear.
But sacred Freedom, too, was theirs;
If thou'rt a slave, indulge thy sneer.[6]

CHAPTER TWO

By The Waters of Doon

Ye flowery banks o' bonie Doon
How can ye blume sae fair;
How can ye chant, ye little birds,
And I sae fu' o' care!

The Banks o' Doon

This was Mount Oliphant, a farm of seventy Scots acres which
lay some two miles south-east of Alloway, high above the waters
of the Doon.

Dirt and Deity
A Life of Robert Burns by, Ian McIntyre.

As their family duly increased William and Agnes Burnes were faced
with the problem that the cramped cottage at Alloway was no longer
providing a comfortable lodging for them all. Besides, William had
demanding ambitions; his scheme to establish a market garden in the land
he leased around the cottage had not exactly prospered, and although he
was grateful enough to fall back on his employment as Provost Fergusson's
head gardener in the meantime, he began to reason that his future prosperity
lay in farming. He decided to unload part of his leased land around the
cottage, but retained a good five acres for his immediate needs.

In the autumn of 1756, and Robert now aged six, Burnes managed to
come-by the opportunity he sought. His employer, William Fergusson, had
again added to his ever expanding estate by purchasing the small farm of
Mount Oliphant, approximately two miles south-east of Alloway, and a
half-mile east of the River Doon. William approached him with a view to
renting the farm, and agreed terms on the basis of a twelve year lease: £40
per annum, for six years, thereafter rising to £45 for the remaining period.
It was no bargain! Richard Fowler, whose scholarly study of Burns has
provided the best available information, within the poet's story, regarding
18th century agriculture, summed up the Mount Oliphant venture by
commenting:

From scraps of information available to us today it would appear that William Burnes's Mount Oliphant landlord, Dr Fergusson, was a kindly fellow and well disposed towards his conscientious tenant. However, as a successful medical man retiring from his London practice to settle in Ayr, his knowledge of farmland improvement was sadly lacking. True, he did advance £100 to William for the purchase of a few cows and horses, but he was mistaken if he believed that unimproved Mount Oliphant would earn him a continuing rental of £40 rising to £45 annually, and comfortably support a tenant with a large and growing family. The land demanded substantial capital for improvements which liming and drainage could effect; capital which he - not his tenant - should have provided. Enlightenment on such essentials had not come to Dr Fergusson, although it was already paying off for many landlords.[1]

Although the lease was agreed to run from November 1765, it was not until the following spring or early summer that the family were able to move into the farmhouse. By this time Robert and Gilbert were both receiving some elementary schooling at Alloway. They had been enrolled at a small country school at Alloway Mill, close by the estuary of the River Doon, run by William Campbell. This school had opened in early 1765, but within a few weeks Campbell accepted the offer of work, in Ayr, and promptly closed his enterprise. However, another teacher, John Murdoch, a local youth who had studied at Ayr Grammar, and completed his education in Edinburgh, made his services available to Burnes and a few other parents in the area, by the month of May in the same year.

When Burnes took his family to Mount Oliphant in the following year it meant that his two sons had to walk from the farm to Murdoch's school, which was situated only a short distance from their former home at the Alloway cottage. Murdoch, incidentally, pompously described the cottage in later life to Dr Currie, as, an "argillaceous fabric," whilst adding that the parents of his pupils took it in turns to provide his accommodation. Of his famous pupil, John Murdoch has supplied posterity with his opinion thus:

Robert Burns, was then between six and seven years of age; his preceptor about eighteen. Robert, and his younger brother Gilbert, had been grounded a little in English before they were put in my care. They both made a rapid progress in reading, and a tolerable progress in writing. In reading, dividing words into syllables by rule, spelling without book, parsing sentences, &c.,

Robert and Gilbert were generally at the upper end of the class, even when ranged with boys by far their seniors.....

Gilbert always appeared to me to possess a more lively imagination, and to be more of the wit, than Robert. I attempted to teach them a little church-music. Here they were left far behind by all the rest of the school. Robert's ear, in particular, was remarkably dull, and his voice untunable. It was long before I could get them to distinguish one tune from another. Robert's countenance was generally grave, and expressive of a serious, contemplative, and thoughtful mind.[2]

Whatever Murdoch may have thought of his pupil's lack of musical ability, Robert, from an early age, appears to have responded with real delight to his mother's singing of the many old ballads which circulated around the Ayrshire countryside at that time - her own favourite carried the lines:

> Kissin is the key o' love,
> An clappin is the lock,
> An makin o's the best thing
> That e'er a young thing got.

Another one which always pleased her eldest son was called *The Life and Age of Man* - Agnes, as a young woman, had frequently sung this to her old blind uncle who had lived with her and her grandmother at Maybole; the poor fellow, as often as not, shedding tears at the sad refrain of the verses:

> 'Twas in the sixteenth hunder year
> Of God and fifty-three
> Frae Christ was born, that bought us dear,
> As writings testifie;
> On January the sixteenth day,
> As I did lie alone,
> With many a sigh and sob did say,
> Ah! man was made to moan!

Many years were to pass ere Robert Burns decided that the phrase: "Man was made to moan", sounded rather better when amended to, "Man was made to mourn".

In addition to the pleasure of listening to his mother's singing, Robin, as his family called him, delighted in the collection of stories related by old Betty Davidson, who had been married to his mother's cousin - now widowed, she resided with the Burnes family, assisting Agnes with the running of the household. She apparently provided Robin, and the others, with endless hours of incredulous folklore tales, much to their great amusement: devils, ghosts, fairies, brownies, witches, kelpies, elf-candles, apparitions, cantraips, dragons, - they were, one and all, traipsed out, bound in a mesh of superstitious nonsense; yet, they left such an impression on Robert that he later confessed:

> This cultivated the latent seeds of Poesy; but had so strong an effect on my imagination, that to this hour, in my nocturnal rambles, I sometimes keep a sharp look-out in suspicious places; and though nobody can be more sceptical in these matters than I, yet it often takes an effort of Philosophy to shake off these idle terrors.[3]

From childhood Robert Burns has a passion for reading that remained with him throughout his life. Comments made by friends who observed him at various stages of his life have suggested that a book was never far from his reach. An early friend, David Sillar, who was favoured with the popular verse epistle, *To Davie, A Brother Poet,* commented that, in a visit to the Burnes household, one was liable to find each member of the family deeply engrossed in a book of their particular choice. Robert himself regarded the first two books he ever read as the ones which gave him the greatest pleasure - no doubt, nostalgia, rather than academic tenure, guided him towards this conclusion - these books were:

> .....the life of Hannibal and the history of Sir William Wallace. Hannibal gave my young ideas such a turn that I used to strut in raptures up and down after the recruiting drum and bagpipe, and wish myself tall enough to be a soldier; while the story of Wallace poured a Scotish prejudice in my veins which will boil along there until the flood-gates of life shut in eternal rest.-[4]

The farm at Mount Oliphant had at least given William Burnes the comfort and staisfaction that he now had the means whereby he could keep his young family as an integral unit under his own roof. He had been concerned that Robert, closely followed by Gilbert, would soon have been of an age when they would have gone out to labour on a neighbouring farm, or perhaps even had to leave the area to obtain work as a live-in gaudsboy (ploughboy) at a distance from home. In 1768 schoolmaster Murdoch received the offer of work at Dumfries, accepted the position, and the little school at Alloway probably closed down; certainly there was no further mention of Robert and Gilbert attending it after Murdoch's departure from the district.

They now spent their days attending what chores their young bodies were capable of on the farm, and in the evenings their father took upon himself the task of teaching them as best he could; arithmetic was later mentioned, by Gilbert, as being the subject that dominated these lessons. Indeed, these little sessions were the only education that the eldest daughters, Agnes and Annabella, ever received. There is no doubt that William Burnes was something of a unique person for his time; John Murdoch was movingly impressed by him, and wrote of him in the most glowing terms, as being among the best of the human race he had ever encountered, and Murdoch could by then list among his acquaintances the famous French statesman, Talleyrand. Quite clearly William Burnes was a devoted husband and a kind, considerate father. Of his seven children, only his daughter Agnes ever felt the weight of his hand in physical chastisement, and that but once - her wilful disobedience when he was teaching her to read, brought her the shock of her father's wrath, and she never again provoked him. His youngest child, Isobel, recalled fond memories of her father's infinite patience when he would sit down by her side in the fields (at Lochlie), and teach her the names of the various grasses and wild flowers. He always came to her when it thundered, being aware of the terrors it held for her.[5]

Shortly before Murdoch left for his teaching appointment in Dumfries, he made his way to Mount Oliphant with the intention of leaving a couple of books as a keepsake, which Gilbert, in his later narrative, recalled as being "a small compendium of English Grammar, and a copy of the play, *Titus Andronicus,*" regarded by some as the work of Shakespeare. This, the schoolmaster decided to read aloud, but when he reached the bloody scene of: "Lavinia, with her hands cut off and her tongue cut out, and ravished", it proved too much for Robert, who boldly announced that if such an awful book was left at his home, he would throw it into the fire.

His father was appalled, and ordered him to remember his manners, but John Murdoch intervened to say that he understood, and if the boy was upset by the language of the play, he would leave another book instead.

Although scarcely ten years of age Robert, guided by his father's assistance, was tackling books on astronomy and natural history. From Stackhouse's *History of the Bible* he acquired, according to Gilbert, "a pretty competent knowledge of ancient history: for no book was so voluminous as to slacken his industry, or so antiquated as to dampen his researches". An uncle, making a visit into Ayr, had been instructed by William Burnes to buy a copy of, *The Ready Reckoner,* and also, *The Complete Letter-Writer,* for the benefit of teaching his youngsters. A mistake was made, and the uncle returned with: "A Collection of Letters by the most Eminent Writers". Whatever Burnes thought of his brother-in-law's error is not known - the wrong book, however, was an apparent delight to his eldest son, who poured endlessly over its pages.

The main concern of William Burnes regarding his attempts at educating his youngsters seems to have centred on the state of their handwriting. In a bid to rectify this he arranged to send Robert and Gilbert, week about, because of the pressure of farming duties, to a school at Dalrymple, a village approximately three miles hence. At this school Burns met James Candlish, whom he later described as the first friend, his brother Gilbert apart, he had made in life. Two letters written to Candlish in 1787, and a letter from him to the poet, are extant. Candlish later studied medicine at Glasgow University, and married a Mauchline girl, Jean Smith, whose brother James was addressed by the poet in one of the best verse epistles he would ever write.

It was during this period that Burns considerably expanded his reading thanks to "a bookish acquaintance" of his father, who loaned him a copy of *Pamela,* by Samuel Richardson, the first novel he ever read; his father also borrowed, on his behalf, a volume on English history for the period of the early 17th century. Gilbert noted that *Pamela* was the only book of Richardson's which Robert read until he turned author himself. In fact, with the exception of two works of Smollett, it appears that Burns really read very little of note, with regard to the eminent contemporary writers, until he had published his own volume of poems in 1786.

He had, however, obtained a copy of Alexander Pope's works, and some other poetry - and this material had come from an unexpected source, in the person of his former schoolmaster, John Murdoch. He had returned to the area to become: "the established teacher of the English language at Ayr, a circumstance of considerable consequence", as Gilbert was to put it. In this same passage of Gilbert's narrative, mention is made of *The Edinburgh Magazine* for the year 1772. It is interesting to note that, from the edition of this journal for 1774, Robert Burns, many years later at the height of his career, copied two songs which he sent into the *Scots Musical Museum,* edited by James Johnson - *Powers Celestial,* and, *Could Ought of Song* - both pieces were published in the fifth volume of the *Museum* which appeared six months after Burns's death, and they were accepted for almost a century, as unquestionably the poet's own verses. In the year 1871, however, the diligence of a certain James Christie, librarian at Dollar Institute, spotted the songs in the 1774 magazine, the result being, as Scott Douglas put it, "the number of Burns' lyrics were lessened by *two.*" When the same editor was preparing his 1877-9 edition of Burns, he was alerted by Christie to the effect that the song, *Behold The Hour,* had been culled out of a sixteen verse poem, *Before The Fatal Hour,* given in the same magazine, to which Burns had made but minor variations. Richard Fowler, following the example of Henley & Henderson, expressed annoyance that Burns had foisted the lyrics off as his own when George Thomson was looking for verses to suit the air, *Oran gaoil.* James Mackay, somewhat more generously, has described Burns's lyrics as: "a Scotticized version of an English song", and this should satisfy all but the most demanding of critics.

There is some indication that, around the period of 1772-4, Robert began to take an active interest in the street ballads which were printed out and sold cheaply in the market stalls. It was also during the year 1773 that his father decided to take advantage of John Murdoch's return to Ayr, and Robert was sent to board with the young teacher, for several weeks, during which time he appears to have acquired a working knowledge of French:

> Observing the facility with which he had acquired the French language, Mr Robinson, the established writing master in Ayr, and Mr Murdoch's particular friend, having himself acquired a considerable knowledge of the Latin language by his own industry, without ever having learnt it at school, advised Robert

to make the same attempt, promising him every assistance in his power. Agreeable to this advice, he purchased *The Rudiments of the Latin Tongue,* but finding this study dry and uninteresting, it was quickly laid aside. He frequently returned to his *Rudiments* on any little chagrin or disappointment, particularly in his love affairs; but the Latin seldom predominated more than a day or two at a time, or a week at most.[6]

John Murdoch found him to be a totally responsive pupil, as he "attacked the French (language) with great courage." However, the demands of Mount Oliphant farm were more pressing than the declension of nouns and conjugation of verbs in French, and the youthful student had to depart for home, where: "armed with a sickle to seek glory by signalizing himself in the fields of Ceres.....although only about fifteen.....he performed the work of a man."

To what extent Burns ever became proficient in French, has been a much debated point. James Mackay, himself a linguist of considerable ability, has concluded that, the occasional French phrases in his poetry, in their context of scansion and rhyme, lies a suspicion that his pronunciation was idiosyncratic; though, as Dr Mackay has noted, the poet took delight in sprinkling his letters with French phrases, and naming French books which he had read, thus indicating that he had a working knowledge of the language.

Although the house in which Burns lodged with Murdoch has long since been demolished, the building which subsequently replaced it was identified with a plaque affixed to its front stating: "Here stood the house of John Murdoch, schoolmaster, in which Robert Burns lodged in his fourteenth year and received lessons in English and French". Another boarder with Murdoch at the same time was, John Tennant, a son of his father's close friend, the farmer of Glenconner - "auld Glen", as Robert would later affectionately address him in a verse epistle sent to James Tennant, the family's eldest son.

CHAPTER THREE

The Sin of Rhyme

This kind of life, the chearless gloom of a hermit with the unceasing moil of a galley-slave, brought me to my sixteenth year; a little before which I committed the sin of RHYME.-

Autobiography

O ONCE I lov'd a bonnie lass,
An' aye I love her still,
An' whilst that virtue warms my breast
I'll love my Handsome Nell.

O Once I Lov'd

In his autobiography Burns has informed us that he "first committed the sin of rhyme" in his fifteenth autumn. He would therefore, have been fourteen years of age, and the year 1773. The background to the song, *O Once I Lov'd a Bonnie Lass,* places the time as late September, and the gathering of the harvest at Mount Oliphant. However, this is somewhat contradicted by his version in the Stair MS where he indicates that the verses were composed a few months after entering his sixteenth year. How far "a few months" would encroach into a year from his January birthday, is anybody's guess:

> You know our country custom of coupling a man and woman together as Partners in the labors of Harvest.- In my fifteenth autumn, my Partner was a bewitching creature who just counted an autumn less.....She was a bonie sweet, sonsie lass.- In short, she altogether unwittingly to herself, initiated me in a certain delicious Passion, which in spite of acid Disappointment, gin-horse Prudence and bookworm Philosophy, I hold to be the first of human joys, our dearest pleasure here below.- .....Among her other love-inspiring qualifications, she sung sweetly; and 'twas her favorite reel to which I attempted to giving an embodied vehicle in rhyme.[1]

It is unlikely that Burns, a competent mathematician, would have miscalculated the precise year of his fifteen autumn, and since the evidence suggests that the harvest gathering was the occasion of him turning poet, the year would have been 1773. The comment in the Stair MS probably indicates that the verses had been neglected after their immediate impact, in the autumn of 1773, until sometime after his fifteenth birthday when, perchance, revision was done on them with perhaps verses added, before they became the finished article. Many years later, in March 1787, the poet recalled his early passion:

> But still the elements o' sang
> In formless jumble, right an' wrang,   (wrong)
> Wild floated in my brain;
> Till on that hairst I said before,   (harvest)
> My partner in the merry core,
> She rous'd the forming strain.[2]

This partner was named only as Handsome Nell; no mention of a surname was made, and her identification, resting on information passed from Isobel Burns to Robert Chambers, claimed her as Nell Kilpatrick, daughter of John Kilpatrick, a miller at Parclewan near Dalrymple. An alternative claim, however, has been lodged on behalf of a certain Helen Blair as the heroine of the song. In an anonymous letter to *The Scotsman*, in 1828, the writer declared that Burns had written the verses in praise of a servant girl who worked at the house of one of his friends, and added that the poet had written several other songs for her, none of which survived. The Revd. Hamilton Paul claimed that he met Handsome Nell in the year 1811, but she apparently made no mention to him of the other songs Burns is alleged to have written. Then, as now, the cloak of anonymity devalues the credibility of any story; and, when the source is further removed to a friend of the informant, as in *The Scotsman* letter, a measure of deep suspicion must inevitably cloud the issue.[3] The gist of the letter presented Burns in a manner which is totally out of character with the information we have of him, from his own pen, and from Gilbert's, regarding this period of his life.

It is certainly true that Isobel Burns, born in 1771, would have been too young to recall the events taking place a mere two or three years later; however, she had quite obviously obtained, over the years, information on her famous brother's younger years, given to her by their mother, by Gilbert, and by her elder sisters. Such information is now as close as we can get to the established truth, outwith positive written statements from unequivocal sources. Chambers knew Hamilton Paul; he also knew of *The*

Scotsman letter, and he was prepared to reject such claims in favour of the name given by Burns's sister - there is no real reason to doubt his judgement! Thus, the partner who sang her favourite reel to the young Burns as they gathered the harvest, must be assumed as Nell Kilpatrick, and to her falls the honour of being the first of the poet's heroines. The tune which she lilted to Burns, *I Am a Man Unmarried,* had long been regarded as, "irretrievably lost"; however, the *Weekly Scotsman* published a communication sent to them, in March 1925, by George St. J. Bremner, of San Fransisco, who had recalled his grandfather singing it some sixty years previously. He supplied the 'paper with a copy of the music, adding that: "When played in reel time, it made a capital dance tune."[4]

According to his autobiography Burns, some two years after his first poetic attempt, decided to give his "manners a brush" by enrolling at a country dancing-school; he added that he did so, in "absolute defiance" of his father's orders; a stance of which he later expressed much regret. The summer of the same year was spent at Kirkoswald, if Robert's text is accurate! The original letter to Dr Moore, now in the keeping of the British Museum, carries an amendment, assumed to be on his brother's authority, that shunts the Kirkoswald period at least two years forward to 1777. At any event, his duration on the Carrick coast "made very considerable alterations to (his) mind and manners", and not only in the specific nature of the exercise for which it had been arranged - the study of 'Mensuration, Surveying, Dialling &c,' - he seemed satisfied enough with his progress in these subjects; but he also claimed, "even greater progress in the study of mankind."

At this particular time Kirkoswald was thriving on the illicit trade of smuggling. The nooks and coves of the surrounding shoreline proved a perfect location for landing contraband goods from France via the Isle of Man; brandy was, apparently, shipped ashore flowing in abundant quantities. It was during his stay at Kirkoswald, that Robert Burns made the startling discovery that he was "no enemy to social life" declaring in his autobiography:

> The contraband trade was at that time very successful, and it sometimes happened to me to fall in with those who carried it on. Scenes of swaggering riot and roaring dissipation were, till this time new to me; but I was no enemy to social life. Here,

though I learnt to fill my glass, and to mix without fear in a drunken squabble, yet I went on with a high hand with my geometry, till the sun entered Virgo, a month which is always a carnival in my bosom, when a charming *fillette* who lived next door to the school, overset my trigonometry, and set me off on a tangent from the sphere of my studies. I struggled on with my *sines,* and *co-sines,* for a few days more; but stepping out to the garden one charming noon to take the sun's altitude, there I met my angel,

> "Like Proserpine gathering flowers,
> Herself a fairer flower."[5]

The references to filling his glass and mixing in drunken squabbles have generally been dismissed as mere swaggering bravado, the more so by editors and biographers determined to have us believe that Burns was "a veritable model of sobriety" throughout his life. Yet, there is no reason at all for doubting these statements; after all, he considered them important enough to place on record in his autobiography. In this first flush of early manhood, temporarily freed from the immediate gaze of his protective father, and, caught-up with the elements of *crude humanity* who obviously fascinated him, it is perfectly feasible that he fell in with their ways, and gloried in downing his drams with them. It is ridiculous that some writers have branded Burns a swaggering braggart, and, be it said, a blatant liar, in order to protect him from his own testimony of drinking with the rogues of Kirkoswald.

The objection that he lacked the funds to pick up large tavern bills may be overruled when a study is placed on his statement that: "it sometimes happened to me to fall in with those who carried it on."[6] Dare it be suggested that he, who later took the exciseman's oath, had, at Kirkoswald, been in the ranks of the pursued? His tavern bills may well have been financed by occasionally involving himself, in some capacity, within the activities of the contraband trade.

The "charming fillette" who so upset the young poet's studies was Peggy Thomson - the heroine of his verses - *Song, Composed in August,* alluded to by Burns himself as "the ebullition of that passion which ended the school-business": although it is more than likely that the song was written sometime after the Kirkoswald period:

Now westlin winds, and slaught'ring guns
　Bring Autumn's pleasant weather;
The moorcock springs, on whirring wings,
　Amang the blooming heather:
Now waving grain, wide o'er the plain,
　Delights the weary Farmer;
The moon shines bright, as I rove at night,
　To muse upon my Charmer.[7]

His sister Isobel later claimed to have seen a MS in which the above verse ended: "To muse on Jeanie Armour", and this has been partly corroborated from other sources; the text given in all the main editions, however, acknowledges Peggy as the song's heroine.[8]

The return to the relative calm of Mount Oliphant must have taken place at the beginning of September, the sun enters Virgo on 23 August, and Burns refers to spending only a few days more, plus the following week, before his Kirkoswald interlude concluded, in what he reflected upon as a reasonably satisfying exercise:

> I returned home very considerably improved. - My reading was enlarged with the very important addition of Thomson's and Shenstone's works; I had seen mankind in a new phasis; and I engaged several of my schoolfellows to keep up a literary correspondence with me...I had met with a collection of letters by the Wits of Queen Ann's reign, and I pored over them most devoutly.- I kept copies of my own letters that pleased me, and a comparison between them and the composition of most of my correspondents flattered my vanity.- *(Autobiography)*.

None of the letters written at that period have survived; however, three written to John Niven, and a further three to Thomas Orr who were fellow-pupils of Burns at Rodger's school are extant: the earliest of these, addressed to Niven, was dated 29 July 1780. The first of the Orr letters, 7 Sept. 1782, turned up in a package of papers, passed down from Orr's descendants, towards the end of the 19th century. The package also included scraps of verse, not in Burns's handwriting - these have been rejected by most authorities as not being his compositions, though James Mackay has ventured the opinion that he is not so sure that Burns's authorship ought to be dismissed:

> While the sons of debauch to indulgence give way,
> And slumber the prime of their hours,
> Let us, my dear Stella, the garden survey
> And make our remarks on the flowers.
>
> Though Venus herself from her throne should descend,
> And the Graces await at her call,
> To thee the gay world would with preference bend,
> And hail thee the violet of all.

The songs which have been ascribed to Burns during the period of his late teens include: *I Dream'd I Lay; Tibby, I Hae Seen the Day;* and, *The Ruined Farmer.* A fragment of blank verse, which he later recalled from memory, brought the comments:

> In those days I never wrote down anything; so, except a speech or two, the whole has escaped my memory. The following, which I most distinctly remember, was an exclamation from a great character - great in occasional instance(s) of generosity, and daring at times in villainies.- He is supposed to meet with a child of misery, and exclaims to himself -
>
> All devil as I am, a damned wretch,
> A harden'd, stubborn, unrepenting villain,
> Still my heart melts at human wretchedness;
> And with sincere tho' unavailing sighs
> I view the helpless children of Distress.
> With tears indignant I behold th' Oppressor,
> Rejoicing in the honest man's destruction,
> Whose unsubmitting heart was all his crime.[9]

The fragment runs to twenty lines in total, and was never worked into its intended Tragedy, the explanation being that, "the bursting of a cloud of family Misfortunes, which had for some time threatened us, prevented my further progress." The misfortunes referred to by Burns, concerned the growing crisis emanating from the constant struggle of trying to make Mount Oliphant a profitable enterprise, and of the noticeable effects that the constant strain of this was having on his father's health. When their landlord, William Fergusson, Provost of Ayr, died on 7 November 1776, ten years after agreeing to rent the farm to William Burnes, the lease had a further two years to run. The Fergusson family put the matter into the hands of a factor who appeared to act in an over zealous-manner, extending neither sympathies for adversities encountered by Burnes, nor patience regarding overdue rent:

> My father's generous Master died; The farm proved a ruinous bargain; and, to clench the curse, we fell into the hands of a Factor who sat for the picture I have drawn of one in my Tale of two dogs.- My father was advanced in life when he married; I was the eldest of seven children; and he, worn out by early hardship, was unfit for labour....We lived very poorly; I was a dextrous Ploughman for my years; and the next eldest to me was a brother, who could drive the plough very well and help me to thrash.- A Novel-Writer might perhaps have viewed these scenes with some satisfaction, but so did not I: my indignation yet boils at the recollection of the scoundrel tyrant's insolent, threatening epistles, which used to set us all in tears.
>
> *(Autobiography).*

> I've notic'd, on our Laird's *court-day,*
> An' mony a time my heart's been wae,   (vexed)
> Poor *tenant-bodies,* scant o' cash,
> How they maun thole a *factor's* snash;   (must) (sneers)
> He'll stamp an' threaten, curse an' swear,
> He'll *apprehend* them, *poind* their gear,   (Impound their
> While they maun stand, wi' aspect humble,   stock)
> An' hear it a', an' fear an' tremble![10]

The poet's younger brother Gilbert recorded an equally stark picture regarding their way of life at this farm, stating that the hardships endured by William Burnes and his family caused Robert and himself "the deepest distress." Unlike Robert, however, he made no mention of the "factor's snash" - but then, the timid Gilbert never could summon the courage to challenge the arrogance of his so-called social betters!

In the end, William Burnes did manage to liberate himself from the stranglehold of his lease. Although he was unable to clear some outstanding arrears, a satisfactory arrangement was reached whereby his holding at Alloway was mortgaged until such time as a sale could be arranged. Thus, the evil practice of poinding (seizure of goods and assets under warrant) was, mercifully, avoided. It was unlikely that Fergusson's daughters, the executors of his estate, would have allowed such an act to take place, and they may well have instructed their factor, presumably an Ayr lawyer, to curb his aggressive manner.

The twelve year lease on Mount Oliphant expired at Martinmas (11 November) 1777; the cottage and ground at Alloway were initially rented out, but four years later in 1781, they were finally put on the market for sale, the purchaser, in turn, renting the cottage to a shoemaker who remained under its roof until the beginning of the 19th century. Having bid a none too reluctant farewell to Mount Oliphant, William Burnes negotiated the lease on a larger farm approximately ten miles distant, situated near enough equidistant between Tarbolton and Mauchline - it was named Lochlea, or by its now more commonly known spelling - Lochlie.

CHAPTER FOUR

The Nature of the Bargain

The nature of the bargain was such as to throw a little ready
money in his hand at the commencement, otherwise the affair
would have been impractible.- For four years we lived
comfortably here.

Autobiography

In Tarbolton, ye ken, there are proper young men,
And proper young lasses and a', man:
But ken ye the Ronalds that live in the Bennals,
They carry the gree frae them a', man.

The Ronalds of the Bennals.

The farm at Lochlie was considerably larger than Mount Oliphant
extending to 130 acres, and thus covered an increased area of forty acres
over the previous one. Although the soil was judged to be an improvement
on Mount Oliphant, the undrained loch from which the farm took its name,
tended to give the earth a swamp induced texture. At some four-hundred
feet above sea level it had an elevated site for that particular district of
Ayrshire.

According to Ian McIntyre, it was shortly after the move to Lochlie
in 1777, that Robert's act of defiance against his father took place. The
incident stemmed from the young poet's yearning to stimulate his social life
by attending dancing classes. McIntyre's chronology is no doubt based on
information given by Gilbert and Isobel Burns; however, Robert
specifically stated that he attended the classes in his seventeenth year,
which places it as 1775. He did attend a dancing class in 1778-9, as did
Gilbert, along with their sisters, Agnes and Annabella. This was hardly
likely to be the occasion of Robert earning his father's disapproval
however, since his brother and sisters, who were also involved, seemingly
were not rebuked. The annoyance of Burnes towards Robert's dancing must
have taken place during the Mount Oliphant period, and their father had,
presumably, mellowed in his attitude by the time of the dancing classes at
Tarbolton some three years later.

The rent of Lochlie had been negotiated at the round figure of 20 shillings (one pound) per acre, - £130 per annum. It would appear that the new landlord, David McClure, advanced a sum of money to Burnes as working capital to set him off on a fair start; the poet describing the conclusion of the deal as, "a little ready money" coming into his father's hand. The Burnes family, from the outset, were determined to improve the farming potential by removing soil from around the lower reaches of the farm onto the sparse surfaces of the higher lands. McClure kept an extremely observant eye on such activities deemed necessary for improvements. Burnes would later be accused of removing a quantity in excess of an agreed amount.

Meanwhile, Robert Burns, when he could find the time, went about the business of reading every meaningful book he could lay his hands upon. The poetry of Pope, Shakespeare, and Ramsay; the *Spectator;* John Locke; Thomas Stackhouse; and, in addition, Jethro Tull and Adam Dickson in their respective manuals of agricultural improvement. However, a select *Collection of English Songs*, by the authority of his own statement, became his *Vade mecum:*

> I pored over them, driving my cart or walking to labor, song by song, verse by verse, carefully noting the true tender or sublime from affection and fustian.- I am convinced I owe much to this for my critic-craft such as it is. *(Autobiography)*

His *vade mecum* has never been positively identified. There was a publication by the title *Collection of English Songs,* edited by Joseph Ritson, and Burns certainly owned a copy of at least one volume in the three-volume set. Indeed, it has recently been acquired by the National Library of Scotland. In 1928, Robert Dewar, in a letter to the *Times Literary Supplement,* staked his reputation that the copy of Ritson was the book referred to by Burns.[1] Professor Dewar is probably best remembered within Burns circles as the academic who was initially engaged to edit the Oxford University English poets series; alas, ill-health and subsequent death prevented his involvement beyond the stages of research - his successor, as editor of this highly acclaimed work was, of course, James Kinsley. The main stumbling block to accepting the Ritson as the poet's *vade mecum* lies in its publication date of 1783, which seems at considerable variance with the period stated in Burns's autobiography. To identify the book as the

Ritson, it would, therefore, be necessary to assume that Robert had taken quite a liberty in the chronology of his own story.

Of the friends Burns made in the parish of Tarbolton his "brother poet", David Sillar, is the one most readily recalled from this specific epoch. He was the recipient of the well known verses *Epistle to Davie,* (Jan. 1795) and of a further *Epistle* written some eighteen months later. David Sillar has left a vivid pen-picture of the young Burns in his days at Lochlie farm:

> He wore the only tied hair in the parish; and in the church, his plaid, which was of a particular colour, I think *fillemot* (russet), he wrapped in a particular manner round his shoulders. These surmises, and his exterior, had such a magical influence on my curiosity, as made me particularly solicitous of his acquaintance..... After the commencement of my acquaintance with the bard, we frequently met on Sundays at church, when, between sermons, instead of going with our friends or lassies to the inn, we often took a walk in the fields.....Some of the few opportunities of a noontide walk that a country-life allows her laborious sons, he spent on the banks of the river, or in the woods of the neighbourhood of Stair, a situation peculiarly adapted to the genius of a rural bard. Some book he always carried, and read when not otherwise employed.....[2]

Sillar went on to state that Burns had been reading works on the subject of religion that made his neighbours somewhat suspicious of his opinions, and that, "some even avoided him, as an heretical and dangerous companion."

There are two songs of the period; in the first of which Burns took a decidedly satirical view of *The Tarbolton Lasses* - the final two stanzas of this song being directed at "Bessy" one of the five lasses mentioned by him:

As ye gae up by yon hillside	
Spier in for bonnie Bessy:	(call)
She'll gie ye a beck, and bid ye light,	(curtsey)
And handsomely address ye.	
There's few sae bonny, nane sae guid	(good)
In a' King George' dominion;	
If ye should doubt the truth o' this-	
It's Bessy's ain opinion.[3]	(own)

A companion piece is *The Ronalds of the Bennals:* - both compositions are songs, first published in Robert Chambers's edition of 1851, but their respective tunes were not listed, and have never been traced. The Bennals was a farm of approximately 200 acres, situated within five miles distant from Lochlie. It was owned, and worked, by William Ronald, who thus carried the status of a Bonnet-laird (yeoman): he was regarded, in the district, as a man of considerable wealth, and was certainly not the bankrupt referred to in a letter written by Burns many years later. His daughter Jean apparently caught the amorous attention of Gilbert Burns, but the younger brother of the poet was rebuffed - thus Robert himself, in admitting his own inclination towards her sister Anna, was nevertheless, seemingly prepared to deliberately distance himself, in an attitude of proud defiance; the haughty class system, detested by Burns throughout his life, is given an airing in the lines:

> Then Anna comes in, the pride o' her kin,   (family)
>   The boast of our bachelors a', man:
> Sae sonsy and sweet, sae fully complete,   (pleasant)
>   She steals our affections awa, man.

> I lo'e her mysel, but darena weel tell,
>   My poverty keeps me in awe, man,
> For making o' rhymes, and working at times,
>   Does little or naething at a', man.

> Yet I wadna choose to let her refuse,
>   Nor hae't in her power to say na, man,   (have it)
> For though I be poor, unnoticed, obscure,
>   My stomach's as proud as them a', man.[4]

Chambers could give no definite date for the composition of these songs. They are generally assumed, by Chambers, and most other editors, as having been written during the early period at Lochlie. James Mackay, however, ascribes 1784, as the date, but offers no verification for placing them at such a late period. The reference to "our bachelors" is not likely to mean the Bachelors' Club, founded by Burns and some cronies, in November 1780. Had the poet intended this interpretation he would have given bachelors with a capital letter, and probably italicized it in the text.

Another early song was, *O Tibby, I Hae Seen the Day,* the first stanza of which suggests that, the disdainful *Tibby* has snubbed the young poet's friendly salutation to her:

Yestreen I met you on the Moor	(last night)
Ye spak'na but gaed by like stoor	(spoke not) (dust)
Ye geck at me because I'm poor	(glare)
But fien' a hair care I.-[5]	(devil, i.e. damn)

In later times at Ellisland farm, when he annotated Robert Riddell's copy of Johnson's *Scots Musical Museum,* Burns thought he had been about seventeen years of age when he gave *Tibby* her poetic comeuppance; however, Isobel Burns, long after her brother's death, was quite sure that the verses were written at Lochlie; citing as evidence that they were addressed to Isabella Stein, or Steven, whose father's farm 'marched' (adjoined) with their own - the quibble is of no more than a couple of years discrepancy in his age - and that is hardly of any great importance.

The local lasses did not catch all the attention of the spare time he came by when released from farming labours. The founding of the Tarbolton Bachelors' Club was proof enough that Robert and Gilbert had struck up friendships with several young men, who gathered with them in a strictly male-only debating society. The constitution of the Club is extant, and indicates that membership would not be permitted to exceed sixteen; all subjects were to be freely discussed, with the exception of disputed religious opinions; swearing, and profane language were strictly prohibited. Members were instructed not to discuss affairs with outsiders; if they did so, and brought ridicule on another member, the guilty party would be: "for ever excommunicated from the society." The inaugural meeting of the Bachelors' Club was held in a top-floor room of a Tarbolton ale-house, on 11 November 1780, Robert Burns being elected its first president. The MS of the ten drafted rules is not in Burns's handwriting: nevertheless, there seems little doubt that he was their prime author. The concluding rule states:

Every man proper for a member of this Society, must have a frank, honest, open heart; above anything dirty or mean; and must be a professed lover of one or more of the female sex. No haughty, self-conceited person, who looks upon himself as superior to the rest of the club, and especially no mean spirited mortal, whose only wish is to heap up money, shall upon any pretence whatever be admitted. In short, the proper person for this society is a cheerful, honest-hearted lad, if he has a friend that is true, and a mistress that is kind, and as much wealth as genteelly to make both ends meet - is just as happy as this world can make him.

There is no doubt that, ever since his experiences with Nell Kilpatrick in the harvest fields of Mount Oliphant, when his heartstrings thrilled "like an Eolian harp" and his "pulse beat such a furious ratann" when she had him remove the nettle-stings and thistles from her hands, Burns was, well nigh compulsively drawn to the lasses. His early romances would appear to have been little more than teenage flirtations, the most serious of these inflicting no more emotional damage on him than upsetting his trigonometry at Kirkoswald. In the early summer of 1781 this would abruptly change, when he became overwhelmed by the charms of the housekeeper at a nearby country mansion. Only in recent times has this girl's true identity become known: James Mackay, in his celebrated biography of the poet, by astutely delving into the appropriate parish records, and relating them back to other known facts, was able to reveal her as Elizabeth Gebbie, the daughter of a tenant farmer at Pearsland, nearby the village of Galston.

Yet, Burns's own sister had given the name of this "Galston farmer's daughter", as Ellison Begbie, in reply to the enquiries she had received from Robert Chambers, and other writers, anxious for full biographical details of the poet. A genuine mistake - or a deliberate ploy to protect the true identity of Elizabeth Gebbie; perhaps, indeed, at the girl's own request? One writer who actually managed to track her down to her home in Glasgow also allowed the cloak of anonymity to remain more or less intact, despite the fact that he had persuaded her to furnish him with the words of a love-song Burns had written for her some thirty years earlier - *The Lass of Cessnock Banks.* This writer's name was Robert Hartley Cromek, and his book, *Reliques of Robert Burns,* although considerably criticized by subsequent editors of Burns literature, did provide some worthwhile information on the poet which would not have been otherwise available.

CHAPTER FIVE

Montgomerie's Peggy

When o'er the hill beat surly storms,
And winter nights were dark and rainy;
I'd seek some dell, and in my arms
I'd shelter dear Montgomerie's Peggy.-

Montgomerie's Peggy

There had been Peggy too, the self-confident young housekeeper to the gentry up at Coilsfield.....She was dainty, demure, but alas! disdainful in the knowledge that with her dowry she could take her time and make her choice among the best that offered.

The Life of Robert Burns
by, Catherine Carswell.

Down through the years Burns scholars have long pondered over the possibility that Ellison Begbie and Montgomerie's Peggy were one and the same person. Scott Douglas had virtually concluded that they were; however, he then found his researches somewhat stymied by an approach to Isobel Burns requesting confirmation of his findings; the reply from her daughter satisfied Scott Douglas that he had stumbled onto the wrong tracks:

How Mr. D. runs into the mistake of saying that Mrs Begg (Isobel Burns), in her account of Ellison Begbie, represented her as the same with 'Montgomerie's Peggy' is, to me incomprehensible. She has ever said the very reverse; for they were as distinct as two women with two souls can be.

In our own times, James Mackay, having conducted the most detailed researches into this aspect yet accomplished, wrote:

Were it not for Isobel Burns identifying 'Ellison Begbie' and 'Montgomerie's Peggy' as two separate persons, one might suspect that they were one and the same. Both were housekeepers in country mansions.....both had been bred 'in a style of life rather elegant', at least to the extent of being able to read joined-up writing; and both had turned Robert down after being on the receiving end of his billets-doux. .....the admission that 'My Montgomerie's Peggy was my Deity for six or eight months' and the non-existence of any other 'billets-doux' which can be attributed to this girl inevitably leave one wondering.[1]

The 'billets-doux' referred to by James Mackay, were four letters addressed to 'Dear E.' - Although undated, the wording has established that they were composed in the early part of 1781. In the third letter of the series Burns proposed marriage to the recipient; the fourth, and final letter, makes it clear that he was turned down. These letters were published by James Currie in his edition of Burns in the year 1800. They were then withdrawn without comment, in the subsequent editions of Currie, and did not again appear until Allan Cunningham resurrected them for his, *Complete Works of Robert Burns,* published in 1834. The claim, by Cunningham, that Dr Currie seemed to know the lady's identity has been somewhat backed by De Lancey Ferguson's statement: "Currie spelt her Christian name 'Ellison', and has been followed in this by subsequent editors."

When Robert Cromek travelled north to Ayrshire in 1807-8, with a determination to find out all he could about the Scottish poet, the letters to 'Dear E' appear to have caught the attention of his inquisitive nature; he managed to trace her to a house at 74 King Street, in Glasgow, where she now resided, under her married name of Mrs Hugh Brown. During the course of the interview, in this intrusion into her life, Ellison allowed Cromek to write down the words of the song Burns had written about her; a MS of the song turned up much later which verified that Burns was indeed the author.

Yet, despite the trouble he had undoubtedly taken to meet with Ellison, when he published his book of Burns *Reliques,* the only comment made by Cromek in giving the song was a footnote:

This song was an early production. It was recovered by the Editor (Cromek) from the oral communication of a lady residing at Glasgow, whom the Bard in early life affectionately admired.[2]

The song which immediately precedes it in Cromek's book is *Bonie Peggy Alison,* long regarded as lyrics written in praise of Ellison. This song is given in James Johnson's *SMM (No. 193, Vol., II. 1788)* and the original

MS is now lodged in the Hastie Collection of MSS at the British Museum. It has two stanzas and a chorus - an additonal stanza, has long since been given in most editions of Burns, the addendum taken from a collation of Cromek's text, and a later holograph MS which is now filed in the Huntington Library, in California. Where did Robert Cromek obtain the opening stanza? It runs thus:

> Ilk Care and Fear, when thou art near,
> I ever mair defy them, O;
> Young kings upon their hansel throne
> Are no sae blest as I am, O![3]

Although the song is usually titled *Bonie Peggy Alison,* or alternatively from the first line of its chorus, *And I'll kiss Thee Yet,* Cromek chose to list it, in his index as: *Ilk Care and Fear, When Thou Art Near.* There would seem to be only two feasible conclusions as to Cromek bringing this particular verse to light; either he saw a copy of the Huntington MS - and copied it carelessly - or, during the course of his conversation with Ellison, she made mention of it to him.

It was also Robert Cromek who first brought the mysterious 'Montgomerie's Peggy' to public awareness; the lyrics and accompanying annotation formed part of a transcript made from Burns's *Commonplace Book,* which Cromek published in the *Reliques.*[4] From the poet's notes it is known that he wrote this song: "something in imitation of the manner of a noble old Scottish piece called McMillan's Peggy, and sings to the tune of Galla Water." The information on Peggy is decidely scant. She was courted for a period of six or eight months, during which time he sent her several love-letters, all to no avail, as she rejected him in favour of a rival, leaving him admitting the heartaches of the affair. These notes provide the answer to the question raised by James Mackay, as to why he bothered to send letters to a girl living in his own area? Burns frankly confessed that he was showing-off his art in the composition of a *Billet-doux!*

The enigma now surfaces as to whether the letters which Burns admitted sending to Montgomerie's Peggy were the very ones of which draft copies were discovered among his papers by Dr Currie when preparing the first posthumous edition of the poet's works. The obvious stumbling block arises from the given initial of the girl's first name; there is no variant of Peggy that would seemingly justify addressing her as Dear E. Yet, Cromek, who must surely have been aware of this fact, took it upon himself to add a footnote against Burns's annotation of the song: it simply read: "This passage explains the love letters to Peggy." Why was Robert Cromek so sure that the four letters published by Currie were written to Montgomerie's Peggy? One feasible explanation is that she told him so!

The name Peggy was literally forced upon Burns in the two songs, *Bonie Peggy Alison,* and, *Montgomerie's Peggy.* In the former he had, almost certainly, used the chorus of an old song of this title; in the latter he was again constrained by the name, having closely followed, in imitation, another old song *McMillan's Peggy.* Cromek, for his part, would probably have felt obliged to offer some sort of explanation if his footnote had referred directly to the letters to Dear E., considering that the annotation concerned someone named Peggy! He thus chose the convenient way out, and presumably left it to the guile of future scholars to follow his implication.

As to the letters themselves, they have been seen no more since passing through James Currie's editorial clutches - and the transcripts in his four-volume Cadell and Davies publication in the year 1800, remain the only proof of their actual existence. Who knows what became their fate: there remains the possibility that Ellison's attention was drawn to them, and she may have beseeched Currie to refrain from using them further, perhaps even requesting that they be destroyed. As stated, they never again appeared in the subsequent editions of Currie, eight in total, between the period 1801-1820.

The subject of these early love-letters has suffered a further complication by the fact that a fifth letter, in much the same language, came to light and was published in Scott Douglas's edition of Burns in 1878, from a MS discovered by a member of the Greenock Burns Club, John Adam. Where the other letters gave the girl the initial E., this one addressed her as A., and it was generally assumed that she was Alison, or Ellison, depending on personal pronunciation of the name. In his biography of the poet, James Mackay has attempted to put this nonsense to rest, admitting his own error in printing the name Alison in the text of his *Complete Letters of Robert Burns* (Letter No. 5, Alloway Publishing, 1987).[5] No feasible explanation of this letter can now be given; it should certainly not be assumed as part of the series to Ellison Begbie.

The courtship of Ellison did not run smoothly; from the outset it appears that Burns had a rival for her affections and in due course, the poet was informed that she had decided to reject his proposal of marriage, "a peremptory refusal" as Robert styled it. There can be little doubt that, physical attraction apart, Burns was completely captivated by the fact that her intellect placed her well above that of any other young woman who had previously caught his attentions. The closing verse of his *Song of Similes* highlights this point:

> But It's not her air, her form, her face,
>   Though matching beauty's fabled Queen;
> 'Tis the mind that shines in ev'ry grace,
>   An' chiefly in her rogueish een.[6]   (eyes)

There are also several passages in the letters which make it abundantly clear that Ellison's intellect, just as much as her 'sparkling rogueish een', had held the youthful poet in a spellbound anxiety to make her his partner for life:

> All these charming qualities, heightened by an education much beyond anything I have ever met in any woman I ever dared to approach, have made an impression on my heart that I do not think the world can ever efface.[7]

It was during this serious love affair, and whilst his hopes of marrying Ellison were still alive, that Burns began to contemplate the prospects of his future career, with the perpetual problem of how to earn a decent living much to the fore. The lot of a tenant farmer who had no working capital to fertilize, cultivate, and stock his rented holding, had stared him in the face at Mount Oliphant. The same pattern was beginning to emerge at Lochlie. For some time, along with his brother Gilbert he had been using a few acres of farming land specifically for the growing of flax. Burns now contemplated the idea of learning the trade of flax dressing:

> My twenty third year was to me an important era. - Partly thro' whim, and partly that I wished to set about doing something in life, I joined with a flax-dresser in a neighbouring town, to learn

his trade and carry on the business of manufacturing and retailing flax. - *(Autobiography)*

The neighbouring town was Irvine, a royal burgh since the 13th century, and a thriving seaport with a population in excess of 4000, the significance of which is shown when compared with Ayr, in Burns's time, where the population numbered less than 3000. There was, however, a gradual transfer of much of the sea trade up-river to Greenock and Port-Glasgow. Before his departure from Lochlie, Burns was initiated into Freemasonry, at Tarbolton, on the 4 July 1781; he probably set out for Irvine within a week or so of this event. One month before leaving the farm he had written to Willie Niven, a friend from his time spent at Kirkoswald; no mention was made of his forthcoming venture in Irvine, but he did inform Niven:

> I know you will hardly believe me when I tell you, that by a strange conjuncture of circumstances, I am intirely got rid of all connections with the tender sex, I mean in the way of courtship: it is, however certain that I am so; though how long I shall continue so, Heaven only knows; but be that as it may, I shall never be involved as I was again. -[8]

It was an obvious reference to his failed romance with Ellison Begbie. She had, nevertheless, inspired him to write the best songs he had so far produced, *The Lass of Cessnock Banks;* and *I'll kiss Thee Yet;* perhaps also, *Montgomerie's Peggy.* She was, almost certainly, the heroine of his magnificent effusion, *Mary Morison* - Robert Chambers commented on it:

> The view of most biographers and editors is that the words 'Mary Morison' are but a euphonious rendering of 'Ellison Begbie', and that the song of that name was inspired by his first serious passion.[9]

Although Chambers did question this theory on the grounds that, as an art song, *Mary Morison* was vastly superior to anything that Burns had at this period in time produced, the poet himself maintained that it was a product of his early life, and then added the rather astonishing assessment that he: "did not think it very remarkable, either for its merits or demerits." Claims made on behalf of a Mauchline girl named Mary Morison as being the heroine of the verses are, to say the least, spurious. It is, however, quite possible that Burns took the liberty of using her name in lieu of Ellison's, to enhance the quality of the verses. Isobel Burns readily accepted the opinion of Scott Douglas that the early version of her brother's song had concluded each stanza with the name 'Peggy Ellison':

> The idea regarding 'Peggy Ellison' being a euphonious rendering of *Ellison Begbie* is fanciful, but very like truth - O' Peggy at thy window be' - very sensibly arranged by Mr. D.[10]

Gilbert Burns also confirmed this by stating, on being questioned by George Thomson, as to the identity of the girl in the song that: "Mary Morison was the heroine of some old light verses, beginning - *I'll kiss thee yet, yet."* For well nigh two centuries the girl remained shrouded in the mysterious disguise of various names, *Peggy Alison; Ellison Begbie; Mary Morison; Dear E.,* and perchance, *Montgomerie's Peggy* - however, James Mackay, with an excellent piece of literary detective work, finally revealed, beyond reasonable doubt, her true identity as Elizabeth Gebbie, born at Pearsland, near the parish of Galston, on 22 July 1762.[11] Why then had the name Ellison, a most unusual derivative of Elizabeth, been used in the first place? If James Currie really did know the girl by the name Ellison, his information must surely have come from one of two sources; either Gilbert Burns had passed the name on to him, or he found reference to it among the poet's papers. In any event, Isobel Burns later confirmed that Ellison was the name by which she was known to their family, adding that, she married soon after Burns's affair with her terminated.

Isobel Burns attributed her brother's bouts of depression and melancholy moods at Irvine to the fact that his proposal of marriage had been turned down; however, another reason may well have been that the tedious, health-sapping labours of hackling flax were the root casue of what proved to be an non-too-happy period in the young poet's life. To crown it all, the heckling shop caught fire, his possessions were lost in the blaze, and, as described by himself, he was: "left like a true poet, not worth a sixpence". There are two versions of the fire which brought his circumstances to such a sorrowful state. According to Burns it occured whilst they were "giving a welcome carousal to the new year" and it was caused "by the drunken carelessness" of his partner's wife. A long standing Irvine tradition refutes his claim, insisting that Burns had already quarrelled with his partner, had moved out of the shop, and had established premises of his own which were the scene of the fire. It does seem likely that Burns had moved from the heckling shop in the Glasgow Vennel, where he had first worked, to Montgomery Boyd's Close; this being based on the evidence of an Irvine tax ledger which indicated that, 'Robert Burns, flaxdresser', paid seven shillings cess (tax) for the term ending 31 March 1782.

It was during the period in Irvine that Burns encountered the company of Richard Brown, a sailor some six years older than himself. Brown was blamed for doing the young Burns a mischief by convincing him that pre-marital sex was no sin, indeed was one of life's basic joys whenever a compliant girl could be found. Brown vehemently denied this when the story eventually broke in the poet's autobiography. Some writers have actually interpreted this particular part of the text, "...he (Brown) spoke of a certain fashionable failing with levity, which hitherto I had regarded with horror", as meaning that Robert and his sailor friend indulged in what would now be called a gay relationship: such talk is absurd! James Mackay and Ian McIntyre, in their respective biographies, have adequately explained the poet's implication, and when read within its original context, clear of Dr Currie's foolish editorial distortion, it is perfectly plain that Burns was referring to sexual involvement with women, and not with Brown.[12] Nothing further on the matter need now be added here.

CHAPTER SIX

The Poor Man's Dearest Friend

'O Death! the poor man's dearest friend,
The Kindest and the best!
Welcome the hour, my aged limbs
Are laid with thee at rest!

Man Was Made to Mourn.

When my father died, his all went among the rapacious hell-hounds that growl in the kennel of justice.....

Autobiography

Ev'n his failings lean'd to virtue's side

Oliver Goldsmith

By the early part of 1782 Robert Burns had decided to abandon his flax-dressing scheme and return home to Lochlie. By then the "clouds of misfortune" were again striking at the heart of the Burns family, and the poet was aware that his father's health was fast declining due to consumption. The considered opinion that flax should only be grown one year in every four due to its susceptibility to disease, and the need for it to be completely clear of weed infestation, may have persuaded Robert and Gilbert to divert from their original ambitions; the harvest of 1782 appears to have brought down the final curtain on their plans. The sequestration order of May 1783, actually listed: 'Fourteen bundles of shafe lint'.

The litigation trouble which arose at Lochlie stemmed from William Burnes's trusting nature, in which he entered into the long lease of the farm without any written contract being drawn-up. An honest man, he expected others to be equally scrupulous in their word and deed - unfortunately, his landlord, David McClure, lacked such ethics. The surface soil at Lochlie was a sandy clay loam to a depth of around eight inches, a further eight inches brought a mixture hinting at the clay loam which formed by a depth of sixteen inches, and continued to the original till depth of three feet. McClure had commenced a liming programme in 1777 to counter his acid and base depleted soil.

The leasing of the farm to Burnes carried an initial agreement that McClure would provide and spread 100 bolls (approx 10 tons by volume) of Cairnhill lime per acre, and also to make available money for Burnes to spread lime as a second dressing, to an extent of twelve tons of limestone, with coals to burn it down to oxide lime of seven tons per acre. McClure also promised Burnes that he would ensure enclosures to subdivide the farm. In the first four years at Lochlie the ground responded sufficiently with this treatment to allow most of the planted produce a healthy growth. However, when the Ayr bank of Douglas, Heron and Co. began to hit a financial crisis they naturally responded by pressurizing their borrowers, among their number being David McClure - he in turn, seems to have reneged on his promises to William Burnes who, feeling cheated by this action of his landlord, decided to react by withholding a substantial part of the due rent. Real trouble now loomed ominously on the horizon! The dispute was initially referred to arbitration, but the arbiters failed to reach a definite conclusion, and the matter passed into the hands of a certain John Hamilton who was entrusted to deliver the final outcome. He decreed that McClure's claim for £775 was wildly excessive, and immediately ordered that it be reduce to £231. This would, almost certainly, have been acceptable to Burnes, and the matter might have been settled at that juncture; however, further complications now developed when it became known that McClure had mortgaged his estates to John McAdam of Craigengillan, later the recipient of Burns's poem of the opening line: *Sir, o'er a gill I gat your card,* and that McAdam had, in turn, brought legal redress against debtor tenants, including the poet's father. In immediate response William Burnes appealed his case to the Court of Session, where it fell on a legal technicality. Seizing this opportunity McClure stepped in and successfully demanded a sequestration order on all stocks and assets at Lochlie, on the grounds of suspicion that Burnes was preparing to sell-off his crops and livestock. To the family's humiliation the town-crier did his rounds bawling out his explicit warning against buying all goods listed on a compiled inventory. A local scribbler who thoroughly disliked Robert, gleefully wrote:

> He sent the drum Tarbolton through
>   That no man was to buy frae you;   (from)
> At the Kirk door he cry'd it too;
>   I heard the yell;
> The vera thing I write is true,   (very)
>   You'll ken yersel.

There can be no question that McClure's action was completely uncalled for; he had broken his word to William Burnes, and behaved in a manner devoid of basic honour. He had, but occasionally, carried out the intended, and promised, drainage work on the farm; the area named the 'Miln damb' was to remain rent-free until it had been thoroughly drained and limed. In actual fact, no work at all was ever undertaken on it during the period of Burnes's tenancy. The poet's father had no alternative but to return to the court of Session with a counter-action to that of McClure, and the £231 debt was duly awarded to the preferred creditor, the Douglas, Heron and Co. bank, with the order of sequestration checked. The legal costs had all but crippled William Burnes, and his hopes of raising some capital from working the farm were dashed in the misfortune of wretched winter weather. The poet's Australian biographer, the late Richard Fowler, an agriculturalist who became Director of the Science Museum in Victoria, has summarized the situation thus:

> The troubled year of 1783 ended. For unrelieved poignancy the close of the Lochlea scene would outrank that of any Verdi opera. A joyless hogmanay brought to William Burnes only the forebodings of what awaited any eighteenth-century debtor, and prescient fears for the future of his mercurial first-born. Those stresses added their destructive power to the worsening tubercular disorder afflicting him. He died on 13 February, 1784.[1]

Four days later, Robert wrote to his cousin James Burness, a solicitor in Montrose:

> I would have returned you my thanks for your kind favour of the 13th December sooner had it not been that I waited to give you an account of that melancholy event which for some time past we have from day to day expected.- On the 13th Current, I lost the best of fathers. Though to be sure we have had long warning of the impending stroke still the feelings of Nature claim their part and I cannot recollect the tender endearments and parental lessons of the best of friends and the ablest of instructors without feeling, what perhaps, the calmer dictates of reason would partly condemn.[2]

The family took the decision that their father's remains should be interred at Alloway, and so, with his coffin in accordance with an old tradition, secured to poles between two bearing-horses, in tandem, William Burnes made his final journey, along an eight mile stretch of country roads, his family and friends on horseback following in close attendance. Robert made arrangements for a suitable headstone to be erected, and composed an eight-line epitaph; the concluding four read:

> The pitying Heart that felt for human Woe;
>   The dauntless heart that fear'd no human Pride;
> The Friend of Man, to vice alone a foe;
>   'For ev'n his failings lean'd to Virtue's side'[3]

The quotation in the final line, was taken from Oliver Goldsmith's *Deserted Village* - one of his favourite poems. In the aftermath of his father's death, Robert penned this entry in his *Commonplace Book:*

> The following song is a wild Rhapsody miserably deficient in Versification, but as the sentiments are the genuine feelings of my heart, for that reason I have a particular pleasure in conning it over:
>
> My father was a farmer upon the Carrick border O
> And carefully he bred me, in decency and order O
> He bade me act a manly part, though I had ne'er a farthing O
> For without an honest manly heart, no man was worth regarding. O

The full song comprises of nine stanzas, concluding thus:

> When sometimes by my labor I earn a little money, O
> Some unforeseen misfortune comes generally upon me; O
> Mischance, mistake, or by neglect, or my good-natur'd folly: O
> But come what will, I've sworn it still, I'll ne'er be melancholy, O
>
> All you who follow wealth and power with unremitting ardor, O
> The more in this you look for bliss, you leave your view the farther: O
> Had you the wealth Potosi boasts, or nations to adore you, O
> A chearful honest-hearted clown I will prefer before you. O[4]

His *Commonplace Book* had been started one year previously, the first entry, in April, 1783, reading:

> Observations, Hints, Songs, Scraps of Poetry, &c., by Robt. Burness; a man who had little art in making money, and still

less in keeping it; but was, however, a man of some sense, a good deal of honesty, and unbounded good-will to every creature rational and irrational.-

.....it may be some entertainment to a curious observer of human-nature to see how a Ploughman thinks, and feels, under the pressure of Love, Ambition, Anxiety, Grief, with the like cares and passions, which, however diversified by the modes and manners of life, operate pretty much alike, I believe, in all species.

There followed two quotations from the English poet William Shenstone (1714-63) who was obviously much admired by the young Burns. The Lochlie period had broadened his reading of the English poets notably Milton and Pope: Shakespeare was studied in greater depth, and the Scottish poets, Allan Ramsay (1684-1758) and Robert Fegusson (1750-1774) were about to stamp their influence on his future literary ambitions. He had also discovered the philosophy of Adam Smith, and remarked on the excellence of the *Theory of Moral Sentiments;* Smith's treatise on economics he would study at a later date. Another philosopher, John Locke (1632-1704), with his *Essay Concerning Human Understanding,* was read during this period, and had a profound effect on the young poet's thinking on the subject of religion, as, to a lesser extent, did John Taylor's *Scripture Doctrine of Original Sin.*[5]

The perplexing problem which had faced Robert Burns ever since accepting that his father's consumption would inevitably prove terminal, was how best to hold the family unit together. The affairs and disputes that had developed at Lochlie made it clear that the tenancy of that farm would have to expire with William Burnes's death. In November 1783, some three months before their father died, Robert and his brother Gilbert thought it prudent to cast around for the lease of an alternative farm. Their attention centred on a 118 acre site, little more than two miles distant, in the parish of Mauchline. This farm, named Mossgiel, was the property of the Earl of Louden - his lordship, however, entrusted the management of it to Gavin Hamilton, a local lawyer. The Burns brothers concluded their negotiations with Hamilton, agreeing to lease the ground at the rent of £90 per annum. "It was", wrote Gilbert Burns, "an asylum for the family in case of the worst. It was stocked by the property and savings of the whole family, and was a joint concern among us". They also registered the full family as employees of their father, thus ensuring their status as creditors of the estate, and allowing them to transfer some small pieces from Lochlie; it was a move which Hilton Brown, somewhat injudiciously regarded as, "a piece of rather sharp practice." Shortly after the funeral, Robert and Gilbert exposed the clandestine agreement they had negotiated with Gavin Hamilton, and moved the Burns family into their new farm.

When the "surly blast" of November's wind swept across the Mossgiel fields during the first winter spent there, it stimulated Robert to later write one of his best known pieces - *Man Was Made to Mourn*. It takes no stretch of the imagination to reason that the much lamented end of old William Burnes was well to the fore in the poet's mind as he drafted the concluding stanza:

> O Death! the poor man's dearest friend,
>   The kindest and the best!
> Welcome the hour, my aged limbs
>   Are laid with thee at rest!
> The Great, the Wealthy fear thy blow,
>   From pomp and pleasure torn;
> But Oh! a blest relief to those
>   That weary-laden mourn![6]

Hard in the wake of this dirge came another poem which had his late father very much in mind. Fergusson's, *The Farmer's Ingle*, was used as the model for the verses which, arguably, have established Robert Burns as the most popular poet of the common people any country has ever seen. The critics - *Those cut-throat bandits in the paths of fame* - have long dwelled on the badly structured, weak lines of *The Cotter's Saturday Night*, but for just as long, they have been drowned-out by the combined voices of the ordinary man. John G Lockhart, biographer of both Scott and Burns, probably got it just about right when he wrote:

> In spite of many feeble lines and some heavy stanzas, it appears to me that even Burns's genius would suffer more in estimation by being contemplated in the absence of this poem, than of any other single poem he has left us.[7]

The case for the people's choice, based on patriotic sentiment, as opposed to the critical analysis of pragmatic literary merit, is rather succinctly presented by Scott Douglas in his notes:

> The spirit of poetry is akin to that of Religion, and the union of
> the two is, in no human composition, more powerful than in the
> present production. The two concluding stanzas of this noble
> poem, the first being a patriotic apostrophe to Scotland, and the
> last a grand address to the Deity in her behalf, were fervently
> recited by the bard, with head uncovered and kneeling on
> English soil with his face towards Scotland, immediately after
> crossing the Tweed for the first time into the sister kingdom, on
> the morning of Monday, 8th May, 1787, while on his Border tour
> with Ainslie.[8]

O Scotia! my dear, my native soil!
    For whom my warmest wish to Heaven is sent!
Long may thy hardy sons of *rustic toil*
    Be blest with health and peace and sweet content!
And O may Heaven their simple lives prevent
    From *Luxury's* contagion, weak and vile!
Then howe'er *crowns* and *coronets* be rent,
    A *virtuous Populace* may rise the while,
And stand a wall of fire, around their much-lov'd Isle.

O Thou! who pour'd the *patriotic tide,*
    That stream'd thro' great, unhappy Wallace' heart;
Who dar'd to, nobly, stem tyrannic pride,
    Or *nobly die,* the second glorious part:
(The Patriot's God, peculiarly thou art,
    His *friend, inspirer, guardian* and *reward!*)
O never, never, Scotia's realm desert,
    But still the *Patriot* and the *Patriot-bard,*
In bright succession raise, her *Ornament* and *Guard!* [9]

CHAPTER SEVEN

Rob Mossgiel

O, LEAVE novels, ye Mauchline belles,
Ye're safer at your spinning-wheel;
Such witching books, are baited hooks
For rakish rooks like Rob Mossgiel.

O, Leave Novels

The Burnes family in Mossgiel was known to be in penury, yet
tenant farmer, Rab, strutted through Tarbolton and Mauchline
with his hair tied jauntily back to flaunt the fact that he was a
poet, whose verse was good enough to catch the eye of people
who knew about such things.

The Tinder Heart
by, Hugh Douglas

The Mossgiel period in the life of Robert Burns enriched the tombs
of Scottish literature with treasures that had never before been seen, and are
never likely to be repeated. Masterpiece followed masterpiece in a glorious
two-year spell which brought the later praise of Robert Louis Stevenson
that Burns had: "attacked literature with a hand that seemed capable of
moving mountains." True his *magnum opus* the incomparable *Tam o'
Shanter,* did not fall within the parameters of this particular spell, nor did
his two best-known songs, *Auld Lang Syne,* and, *A Red, Red Rose,* but the
free-flowing rhetoric of the verse epistles and anti-clerical satires were
indication enough that the new tenant of Mossgiel farm, would not be long
denied acclaim at national level, as a man of literary genius.

One of his best known verse epistles was addressed to David Sillar,
whom he hailed as: "A Brother Poet". It was his first attempt to write in the
measure of Alexander Montomerie's *Cherry and the Slae,* first printed as
far back as 1597, the structure of the poem being formed in stanzas of
fourteen lines - the first ten being fairly equable, with the final four rising
to a somewhat sustained gallop. The fifth verse in the *Epistle To Davie* is
probably its most popular one in quotations from the poem:

It's no in titles nor in rank;
It's no in wealth like *Lon'on Bank*,
To purchase peace and rest;
It's no in makin muckle, *mair:*   (much, more)
It's no in books; it's no in Lear,   (Learning)
To make us truly blest:
If Happiness hae not her seat
And center in the breast,   (centre)
We may be *wise*, or *rich* or *great*,
But never can be *blest*,
Nae treasures, nor pleasures
Could make us happy lang;
The *heart* ay's the part ay,
That makes us right or wrang.[1]

In a critical study of Burns's works, *The Russet Coat,* Christina Keith thought the poem successful enough until Jean Armour was brought into it - verse 8 - and, "metre and theme crashed precipitately to catastrophic ruin.....For Burns' wife never did go with Burns' poetry. The only song she ever inspired ('O' A' the Airts') was written when she was miles - and months - away from him."[2] A harsh judgement indeed, and, most assuredly, a thoroughly inaccurate one!

Some writers have even questioned that the *Darling Jean* of the eighth stanza was the girl whom he later took as his wife. Their suggestion that she was Jean Gardner, however, is really ill-founded; we can be well nigh certain that the 'Jean' who inspired his style and brought the words of the poem, "skelpin' rank and file", was Armour, and not the Buchanite religious crank, thirteen years older than Burns himself. Two completed MSS of this poem are dated 1st January, 1785, thus making it almost certain that Burns met Armour in 1784 - Henley & Henderson suggested that writers who favoured 1785 had taken little account of the poet's natural flare:

Burns moved to Mossgiel, near Mauchline, in March 1784. Is it consistent with his character to have overlooked the charms of the 'jewel o' them a' for more than a year? If he met her first at a ball in Mauchline in April, must it not rather have been in 1784 than in 1785?[3]

This view was supported by Franklyn Bliss Synder in his highly regarded biography of Burns (1932); however, James Mackay, sixty years later, expressed his reservations on the grounds that Burns would have been too busy with the involvement of settling into his new farm, to have afforded the time off for the traditional race-week dance at the end of April. Although he had entered the farming venture "with a full resolution" of making a real go of it, Robin, let it be said, was never one to subscribe to the idea of all work and no play; therefore, based on "the consistency of his character" and the swaggering thought of announcing his presence to *The Mauchline Belles,* it would seem likely that he met them, one and all, sometime in 1784:

> In Mauchline there dwells six proper young Belles,
>   The pride of the place and its neighbourhood a',
> Their carriage and dress a stranger would guess,
>   In Lon'on or Paris they'd gotten it a':
> Miss Miller is fine, Miss Murkland's divine,   (Markland)
>   Miss Smith she has wit and Miss Betty is braw;
> There's beauty and fortune to get wi' Miss Morton,
>   But ARMOUR's the jewel for me o' them a'.-[4]

Miss Smith's brother James was the man destined to become Burns's closest crony during the Mauchline period, and the recipient of the magnificent verses: *Epistle To James Smith,* a poem written in his favourite "standard Habbie" (standard Rabbie, to some) format, and one which outstrips his stanzas "To Davie" in every detail. Jean Smith later married James Candlish, Burns's boyhood friend; she was seven years younger than both, and lived to the ripe old age of eighty-six. With James Smith and a clerk from Gavin Hamilton's office named John Richmond, joined later by William Hunter, a shoemaker, Burns found himself the unelected, but undisputed leader, of a rebel group of four. They soon became individually, and collectively notorious, among the population around Mauchline. The poem, *Libel Summons,* written in May/June 1786, serving mock summonses to a fictitious Court of Equity, upon 'inhibited' fornicators, gives some indication of their brand of humour and fun.[5]

By the beginning of the year 1785, it could no longer be concealed from his family that he himself was, to use his own phraseology, "a proven fornicator." The woman involved was Bess Paton of Largieside, who had worked at Lochlie farm, usually in a capacity of assisting with the household chores. Her daughter was born on 22 May, 1785; Burns was summoned to do penance before the Kirk Session, and to pay his guinea fee for such sins. The pregnancy of Bess, and the birth of his daughter, whom he quickly described as "Dear-bought Bess", she being named after her mother, drew some clever ribald rhyming from Burns, notably his *Epistle To John Rankine,* and, *The Fornicator,* whilst the poem addressed to his Bastart Wean is an astonishing mixture of total tenderness, and absolute defiance against convention. Her mother was, no doubt, the subject of his bawdy song: *My Girl She's Airy.*

There was never any serious intention that he would marry Bess Paton; his mother thought that he should, and Burns himself, initially reflected that it was, perhaps, the right thing to do; however, Gilbert and his sisters were appalled at the very idea, seemingly regarding her as course and common - Robin was quickly persuaded to their advice on the matter, and his courtship of Jean Armour was, by now, paramount. At around the time of his daughter's birth, he was recording in his *Commonplace Book:*

> Tho' mountains frown and desarts howl,
> And oceans roar between;
> Yet, dearer than my deathless soul,
> I still would love my Jean.[6]

The great poems too were now consistently rolling from his pen. Three epistles to elderly John Lapraik, the farmer bard of Muirkirk, who had married the sister of John Rankine; an epsitle to John Goldie, in Kilmarnock, the "terror o' the Whigs"; the verses which immortalized a mouse whose nest his plough had disturbed; the breathtaking splendour of *The Vision,* and the traditions of an Ayrshire *Halloween.* The anti-clerical satires also began to appear, with MSS circulating around the district in mocking torment of the conservative faction (Auld Lichts) in the theological dispute which was then in full torrent of bitter rage - Burns wrote:

> I now began to be known in the neighbourhood as a maker of rhymes.- The first of my poetic offspring that saw the light was a burlesque lamentation on a quarrel between two revd. Calvinists, both of them dramatis personae in my Holy Fair...With a certain side of both clergy and laity it met with a roar of applause.- Holy Willie's Prayer next made its appearance, and

> alarmed the kirk-Session so much that they held three several
> meetings to look over their holy artillery, if any of it was pointed
> against profane Rhymers. *(Autobiography)*

The battle lines drawn between the opposing camps centred more or less on the well worn classic dispute of one group determined to hold onto traditional values and beliefs, confronted by others who were equally determined to move with the times. They soon became identified by the names 'Auld Lichts' and 'New Lichts' and the latter acquired a valuable force of propaganda from the poetry of Robert Burns. As John S Clarke, one time Labour MP for Maryhill, put it:

> Burns sent volley after volley into the religious camp until the very name of Rob Mossgiel was sufficient to make the sweat ooze from the pores of an Auld Licht preacher. His withering ridicule of the Mauchline Holy Fair was instrumental in putting an end to that yearly debauch, mental and physical. From contemporary prose accounts we know that Burns' portrayal of the scene is not one tittle exaggerated. In the "Ordination," "The Epistle to Simson," and the "Dedication," we have three more trenchant attacks delivered against bestial superstition; whilst in the "Cotter's Saturday Night" the humble cottage piety is exalted before all churchcraft of whatever denomination.[7]

Little wonder that the God-fearing James Armour had warned his daughter Jean to steer well clear of the infidel of Mossgiel, and his cronies, Smith and Richmond. The warning went unheeded, and by the early days of 1786 Jean Armour knew she was pregnant. She readily agreed to Burns's proposal of marriage, even though it lacked the blessing of the Church, and merely came in the form of a written declaration drawn-up and signed to effect by the poet, with Smith possibly adding his name as a witness. The real problem confronting Jean, however, was in having to break the news to her father that, not only was she pregnant - she was now, apparently, married to Robert Burns![8] When she did summon the courage to inform him, James Armour is said to have fainted clean away - but soon recovered to announce that, if need be, he would move heaven and earth if necessary, to remove the stain of Rob Mossgiel entering the family as his son-in-law.

Jean Armour was six years younger than her husband, her date of birth variously given as 16 and 25 February, 1765; she was baptized on 3

March, same year. Accounts of her suggest that she was slightly under average height, pretty, rather than a beauty in her youth, dark eyed, with a clear complexion, and a shapely, but rotund, figure; she was certainly literate, but not at all much of a reader. Robert Louis Stevenson, greatly angered the bardolaters with his suggestion that she was "a facile, empty-headed girl" who, after a brief and silly flirtation, trapped Burns into a disastrous marriage.[9]

A showdown with the Armours became inevitable. On the 14 April, 1786, James Armour consulted a lawyer in Ayr, Robert Aiken, with a view to having the marriage annulled - Aiken was the very man to whom Burns had dedicated his poem: *The Cotter's Saturday Night* - "What Aiken in a cottage would have been". The lawyer apparently decided that the best action he could take was to cut away the names on the Burns-Armour marriage lines, presented to him by Jean's father. Burns's biographer, Ian McIntyre, thought: "It all sounds very odd. It is certainly not the sort of thing the Law Society of Scotland would look kindly on today." McIntyre echoed the opinion of many others in assuming that Aiken had given fiery old Armour "the legal equivalent of a placebo", and, in effect, that it succeeded. At any rate, an obviously distressed Burns wrote to Gavin Hamilton:

> Apropos, old Mr. Armour prevailed with him to mutilate that unlucky paper, yesterday.- Would you believe it? tho' I had not a hope, nor even a wish, to make her mine after her damnable conduct; yet when he told me, the names were all cut out of the paper, my heart died within me, and he cut my very veins with the news.[10]

The reference to Jean Armour's "damnable conduct" was prompted by the fact that Burns held her responsible for not standing-up to her parents; for having handed over the marriage lines he had given her, thus allowing her father to put them into Aiken's hands, and for agreeing to leave Mauchline, for the time being, to stay with relatives in Paisley. As far as Burns was concerned, whatever the true legality of the matter, he had now returned to bachelor status, and he saw no reason why he should not act accordingly - barely a month later he even admitted that:

> A storm naturally overblows itself.- My spent passions gradually

sank into a lurid calm; & by degrees I have subsided into the time-settled sorrow of the sable widower, who, wiping away the decent tear, lifts up his grief worn eye to look - for another wife.[11]

Two other schemes were also dominating his line of thought. Gilbert Burns stated that, when Armour's pregnancy became known, Robert, aware that his present financial position would not have supported a wife and child, contemplated going to the West Indies in the hope of securing a better future for them. His emigration plans now seemed to blend with his literary ambition.

I gave up my part of the farm to my brother, as in truth it was only nominally mine; and made what little preparation was in my power for Jamaica.- Before leaving my native country for ever, I resolved to publish my Poems....
....I was pretty sure my Poems would meet with some applause; but at the worst, the roar of the Atlantic would deafen the voice of Censure, and the novelty of west-Indian scenes make me forget Neglect.- *(Autobiography)*

It was during this time, and the thoughts of venturing into "guid black prent" that he composed the *Epistle To James Smith,* in which, incidentally, James Mackay rightly notes that: "Burns develops his rip-roaring denunciation of the censorous, hypocritical bigots of the period." Stanzas six to nine are here quoted.

> The star that rules my luckless lot,
> Has fated me the russet coat,
> An' damn'd my fortune to the groat;
>   But, in requit,
> Has blessed me with a *random-shot*
>   O' countra wit.

> This while my notion's taen a sklent,   (taken a whim)
> To try my fate in guid, black *prent,*   (print)
> But still the mair I'm that way bent,
>   Something cries, 'Hoolie!   (Pause)
> 'I red you, honest man, tak tent!   (warn) (take heed)
>   'Ye'll shaw your folly.

> 'There's ither Poets, much your betters,
> 'Far seen in *Greek,* deep men o' *letters,*
> 'Hae thought they had ensur'd their debtors   (Had)

'A' future ages;
'Now moths deform in shapeless tatters,
'Their unknown pages.'

Then farewell hopes o' Laurel-boughs
To garland my poetic brows!
Henceforth, I'll rove where busy ploughs
    Are whistling thrang,   (busily)
An' teach the lanely heights an' howes   (lonely hills and glens)
    My rustic sang.[12]

After Jean Armour left Mauchline for Paisley in April 1786, Burns became involved with the young woman whom he immortalized in song as Highland Mary. The affair was conducted with discreet secrecy, and thus has become the subject of considerable controversy by those who have written on Burns ever since; Scott Douglas arguably supplied the most positive information about her relationship with Burns, prior to the investigative researches done by James Mackay; indeed, the Scott Douglas version probably still has the clearest ring of the truth regarding this remarkable episode.

It seems to have been a fairly brief affair, and they parted on the 14 May 1786, in the vicinity of Failford; Burns gave her a two-volume Bible, and it has been presumed that he received one in return. Mary returned to her parents' home in Campbeltown shortly after their parting. She died, at Greenock, on, or around, 20 October same year, whilst staying at the home of her mother's cousin; she had been on her way to take up employment as a domestic servant in Glasgow.

By the end of July Burns found himself confronted by further troubles. He had hopes that his emigration plans would shortly take him across the Atlantic, and even announced in a letter to John Richmond, who had left Mauchline to work in Edinburgh, that they "would never meet in Britain more." In the same letter he related that James Armour was now pursuing him, at law, for maintenance of his yet unborn grandchild:

> Would you believe it? Armour has got a warrant to throw me in jail till I find security for an enormous sum.- This they keep an entire secret, but I got it by a channel they little dream of; and I am wandering from one friend's house to another, and like a

true son of the Gospel, 'have nowhere to lay my head'.- I know you will pour an execration on her head, but spare the poor, ill-advised girl for my sake; tho', may all the Furies that rend the injured, enraged Lover's bosom, await the old harridan, her Mother, untill her latest hour![13]

This letter to Richmond was written from Old Rome Foord, indicating that one of the places where Burns chose to hide-out, was the home of the Allans, his uncle and aunt in Dundonald Parish. Their son, Robert Allan, had been employed as a ploughman at Mossgiel.

The 'channel' who had informed Burns of Armour's intention may well have been Jean; whoever it was allowed Burns the opportunity to thwart Armour by transferring his assets, in a deed of assignment, in favour of his brother Gilbert. In return, Gilbert had agreed to foster Robert's illegitimate daughter, Bess, until she reached the age of fifteen. In addition, the copyright of the book of poems, now being published at Kilmarnock, was to be held in her trust until she attained that age. For Jean Armour and child - as it turned out she had twins - there was no arranged provision!

The book, universally acknowledged as the *Kilmarnock Edition* proved to be a tremendous success. It contained thirty poems, including seven verse epistles; three songs; his "Farewell" to the brethren of his Masonic Lodge in Tarbolton; several epitaphs, the final one being, *A Bard's Epitaph,* which concluded:

> The poor Inhabitant below
> Was quick to learn and wise to know,
> And keenly felt the friendly glow,
>   And *softer flame,*
> But thoughtless follies laid him low,
>   And stain'd his name!
>
> Reader attend - whether thy soul
> Soars fancy's flights beyond the pole,
> Or darkling grubs this earthly hole,
>   In low pusuit,
> Know, prudent, cautious, *self-controul*
>   Is Wisdom's root.[14]

The first poem in his book, *The Twa Dogs,* was a clever, imaginary dialogue between two animals, comparing their own, and their respective owners' lifestyles. The working collie, Luath, was based on the farm dog at Lochlie; the pedigree animal, Ceasar, was a Newfoundland, grateful enough to be kept in a spoiled manner, out of pleasure to the gentry who owned him. As it turned out Burns himself, during his tenancy at Ellisland farm, acquired a Newfoundland. He named the dog Thurlow, after the Lord Chancellor in Pitt's government - the large brute frequently accompanied its master when he rode across the countryside on his exciseman's business.

His most accomplished production to date, had been a deliberate omission - a cantata entitled, *Love and Liberty,* or the alternative title preferred by many, *The Jolly Beggars.* Also missing was the savage satire, *Holy Willie's Prayer,* and the holy rumpus between the Calvinist clergymen which had furnished the mirth of *The Twa Herds.* The decision on which pieces to include, and the ones that must fall, was largely political; Burns was shrewd enough to know what his patrons, and future patrons, would stand for, and what could encroach on the boundaries of their toleration - it was, after all, 18th century Scotland: sentiments about churches being "built to please the Priest", and swipes at fundamental Calvinism sending "ane to heaven and ten to hell", were liable to raise many a disapproving eyebrow in influential circles. The poetry that would ensure his future reputation, whether published or not, had by now been written, the only major exception was *Tam o'Shanter,* still some four years off. His career as a poet was virtually at an end - his future literary work would be dedicated to songwriting. He was still only twenty-seven years of age, and wondering if the destiny that lay before him, would keep him in Mauchline, or send him to distant Jamaica.

CHAPTER EIGHT

Farewell To Ayrshire

Farewell, my friends! farewell, my foes!
My peace with these, my love with those -
The bursting tears my heart declare,
Farewell, the bonie banks of Ayr.

The Gloomy Night Is Gathering Fast.

I had taken the last farewel of my few friends; my chest was on
the road to Greenock; I had composed my last song I should
ever measure in Caledonia, "The gloomy night is gathering fast,"
when a letter from Dr Blacklock to a friend of mine overthrew all
my schemes by rousing my poetic ambition.

Autobiography

The affair with Jean Armour, and the subsequent irregular, but
possibly legal marriage, had collapsed in failure, leaving Burns feeling
thoroughly distraught. He admitted to a friend that he had involved himself
in "all kinds of dissipation and riot, Mason meetings, drinking matches, and
other mischief," to drive her out of his head, but all in vain - his poem, *The
Lament,* which he included in the *Kilmarnock Edition,* expressed his
feelings - whilst his *Autobiography,* penned in the following year, reflected
on the event thus:

'Twas a shocking affair, which I cannot yet bear to recollect; and
had very nearly given (me) one or two of the principal
qualifications for a place among those who have lost the chart
and mistake the reckoning of Rationality.-

He had, in effect, attempted to replace the estranged Armour by
turning his amorous attentions on Highland Mary; and, when she left the
area in mid-May, Robin, ever fretful for the companionship of the fair sex,
appears to have taken up with another of the "Mauchline Belles" -
Elizabeth Miller. She had been "the tenant of (his) heart" in the previous
year, but had eventually lost out to Armour. Burns's biographer, Ian
McIntrye, has, incidentally, completely misinterpreted the poet's statement
regarding Elizabeth Miller, citing her sister Helen as "the tenant", then
adding that she had rejected him. The facts, as given by Burns, tell a

different story. At any rate, he managed to include a song for Elizabeth Miller in his *Kilmarnock Edition,* which announced his intention of emigrating:

> From thee, ELIZA, I must go,
>   And from my native shore:
> The cruel fates between us throw
>   A boundless ocean's roar;
> But boundless oceans, roaring wide,
>   Between my Love and me,
> They never, never can divide
>   My heart and soul from thee.[1]

According to James Mackay this song, *Farewell To Eliza,* was written in 1781, out of compliment to Elizabeth Gebbie - indeed, Mackay emphasizes the point by stating it on no fewer than five separate occasions, inferring that all the previous editors had made a hash of the facts.[2] Editors of the calibre of Robert Chambers, Scott Douglas, and above all, the astute William Ernest Henley, were not in the habit of making such elementary errors. Mackay's claim that Burns told Dr Moore that he had written the song before 1782, simply does not ring true. What Burns actually told Moore was, that he had written the first three songs in his book before his twenty third year - this puts an entirely different complexion on the matter. Moore had informed Burns, by letter, at the end of May, 1787, that he had obtained a copy of the poet's latest book - the *Edinburgh Edition* - published in the April of that year; thus, when Burns replied, commenting on his first three songs - he specifically meant the songs in his latest book - the fact that *John Barleycorn* is mentioned in the same paragraph, expels any lingering doubts as this ballad was not included in Burns's *Kilmarnock Edition.* In any case, the internal evidence of *Farewell To Eliza* makes it quite clear that the song has nothing whatsoever to do with Elizabeth Gebbie. Mackay's added comment that there was never any affair with Elizabeth Miller, is refuted by Robert's own statement that she was "the tenant of (his) heart," and also his description of her as his "quondam Eliza". The suggestion, by Mackay, that this alluded to Bess Paton, can be swept aside as utter nonsense!

On the last day of July 1786 the poetry of Robert Burns appeared in "guid black prent"; the "blue-paper boarded thin octavo volume of 'Poems

Chiefly in the Scottish Dialect' was issued to eager crowds of subscribers as fast as Wee Johnnie's folders, stitchers, and binders could get through their work." The book led off with the class-conscious dialogue between "The Twa Dogs" and closed with a Glossary, added for the benefit of those not over-familiar with the Scottish dialect. Ian McIntyre had no hesitation in naming the poetic gem of the book:

> The one poem above all others in the Kilmarnock edition in which Burns went truimphantly right has already been considered. 'The Holy Fair' shows him incontestably at the top of his bent - no stilted neo-classicism here. Effortless and magical, the writing casts its spell from the first stanza. An early critic wrote primly that the poem was 'entitled to every praise except scrupulous decency,' but once again it was Henley who most truly hits the mark: 'I, for my part, would not give my Holy Fair,' he declared 'for a wilderness of Saturday Nights.'[3]

It was, however, the 'Saturday Night' verses which caught the immediate attention of one reader who was, from this period on, to figure with quite an impact in the story of Robert Burns; her name was Frances Anna Dunlop, a member of the Ayrshire gentry, and heiress to the Lochryan estate in Galloway. She was fifty-six years of age when depression as a result of her husband's death in the previous year, and the 'heavy encumbrances' (and mismanagement) had enforced the sale of her Craigie estate. She at once ordered several copies of the *Kilmarnock* and invited the poet to dinner at Dunlop House. His acceptance of the invitation, and their ensuing friendship acted as a great tonic to her, firing her life with a fascinating new interest. For his part Burns was reasonably tolerant of her meddlesome ways, until finally, after some ten years, he dispatched a political bombshell in the form of a letter expressing republican sentiments - she took complete umbrage, and her refusal to reply signalled the termination of their friendship.

The immediate effect of his book was to elevate Burns from the position of a clever local rhymer, to the status of a writer of undoubted national importance. However, his deep personal problems remained, and he was still quite sure that his future lay as a ledger clerk in a slave plantation in Jamaica. On 6 August, 1786, he made the last of three penitential appearances before the Mauchline congregation, having been named to the Kirk Session, by Jean Armour, as the father of her expected child.

He had been due to leave Scotland on, 1 September, 1786, but decided to cancel this sailing date claiming that he had been given insufficient notice. Instead, he spent part of that particular day writing to John Richmond in Edinburgh, giving him a piece of his mind for the fashion in which his friend was treating Jenny Surgeoner, a Mauchline girl who was expecting his child. Two days later Armour gave birth to twins; they were baptized Robert and Jean. It may have seemed rich that Burns could reprimand Richmond, considering his own circumstances, but the situations were not entirely parallel. On the 27th of the same month, Burns again postponed his Jamaican venture: he was obviously now stalling, and seriously wondering if he really should depart old Scotia's shores.

It was a period of much activity for Burns, distributing copies of his book around the district, and collecting much needed payments in respect of same. He was also busy taking his farewells of friends, and according to some sources, he recited his *Farewell to the Brethren of St. James's Lodge Tarbolton,* at one of their meetings, but on what precise date nobody seemed aware. James Mackay states that, tradition maintains it was on 10 November, and this seems feasible. Although by then Burns had abandoned his emigration plans, fate would decree that, shortly afterwards, he did actually take his farewell of Ayrshire. Mackay, incidentally, wrongly states that Burns composed his Masonic *Farewell,* "during this period" (August/September); he had included it in his book, published, of course, in July.

The break of real importance to Burns came from the interest taken in his book by a member of the clergy, Revd. George Lawrie, who was so impressed with the work that he sent a copy to a renowned poet in Edinburgh, old blind Dr Blacklock. Sometime during the latter part of the autumn of 1786 Burns visited Lawrie's manse at Loudoun parish situated above the banks of the River Irvine. On his return home, the poet composed what he thought would be his last song in Scotland: *The Gloomy Night Is Gathering Fast.* Blacklock, as it turned out, asked a favour of his friend, the philosopher Dugald Stewart, to read him Burns's poems, and a few weeks later, on 23 October, Stewart invited the poet to his country home at Catrine House, some three miles south of Mauchline. In the company on that occasion was the young radical aristocrat, Lord Daer, son of the Earl of Selkirk. Catherine Carswell, in her biography of Burns, contrasted the festivities of Catrine House, with a sombre event taking place at Greenock:

> That same afternoon, while the poet was taking wine with Lord Daer at Catrine, earth was being shovelled over the body of Mary Campbell in Greenock churchyard. The same grave contained her dead baby. Round her grave the men of the Campbells and the Macphersons were cursing the name of Robert Burns as the Armours had never cursed it.[4]

It was the first time that the charge was made in print that Mary had, in effect, not died from a raging fever, as previous biographers had claimed, but from the added complications of childbirth. Worse was to come two years later, in 1932, when Franklyn Bliss Snyder's biography, still acclaimed by many as the best ever written on Burns, weighed-in with an echo of Carswell's accusation. It is true that the more cautious Snyder qualified his opinion by: "Assuming for the sake of the argument that this hypothesis is correct"; but his conclusions proved damaging enough that Burns, for the only known time in his life, by his: "lawless love of a woman had cost her her life, and the life of her child."[5]

The arguments, led by Snyder, to the effect that Highland Mary had died in childbirth certainly cannot by registered as conclusive evidence, and, as Snyder himself pointed out, Mrs Carswell had, in effect, issued it as a statement of fact, but offered no real evidence at all - and on this Robert Burns stands accused of a "lawless love" which cost a woman and her child their lives. Much more rational is the opinion of James Mackay who, on a full investigation into all the known facts, concluded with a creditable "not proven" verdict.[6] Some suspicion of Mary's alleged pregnancy stemmed from the tactless comment of Dr Currie who let it be known that he had unearthed some information on the affair, presumably from sifting through Burns's papers, which he thought, "not proper to reveal." Currie ought to have been aware that such remarks would merely excite the gossip of the curious in future years: he should have made known what he knew, or said nothing. In truth, Currie was probably only refusing to release information to the effect that Burns had planned to marry Mary Campbell, a fact confirmed by the poet's youngest sister many years later. It is of no great relevance now; however, at the time, Currie may have felt that it would have embarrassed Burns's widow to make it known that, only because of Highland Mary's tragic death in 1786, had she, Jean Armour, finally attained the designation, Mrs Robert Burns, two years later.

To suggest, as Synder does, that Mary's death was the influential factor in persuading Burns that he no longer had need to flee across the Atlantic is, to say the least, highly debatable. It is most unlikely that Mary Campbell would have sailed with him; no arrangements appear to have been made for her to do so. The song, *Will Ye go to the Indies, My Mary,* is scant proof of any such intentions; yet, on the assumption that he had agreed to marry her, something would surely have been worked out, either to join him later, or await his return when he had earned sufficient funds to furnish their future in Ayrshire.

In his autobiography Burns made no mention whatever of his affair with Mary Campbell, though he wrote it within a year of her death. There is no need to draw any sinister conclusions from this by suggesting, as some have done, that he had something suspicious to conceal. His private grief, and nothing further, may have spurned him from the spectacle of filling the printed page with his public declaration of mourning. Although the autobiography was written initially as a private letter to Dr Moore, there can be no real doubt that Burns was astute enough to know that, in the fullness of time, this document would appear in print, and serve as the basis of biographical details concerning him.

Whether or not Highland Mary's death had any bearing in leading Burns to the decision of staying in Scotland will never be known - what we are left with is this statement that, he was persuaded to abandon the Jamaican project in favour of trying for a second edition of his poems, on the strength of a letter from Dr Blacklock to a friend, which had, he claimed, aroused all his ambitions. In actual fact, Burns kept open his options to emigrate until the very end of the year; his ticket being transferred for a passage on board a ship named *Roselle* sailing out of Leith - a precaution in case matters in Edinburgh did not turn out to his advantage.

His final days at the farm as Rob Mossgiel were busy enough. On 18 November he wrote to Wilhelmina Alexander of the Ballochmyle estate enclosing a song he had composed in her honour. As a member of the local gentry she thought it far too audacious to be so addressed by a mere peasant, albeit, a peasant who was now the author of an acclaimed book of poems. The Alexanders enquired as to who exactly was this Robert Burns - they were not at all impressed by what they heard; so Wilhelmina, the reluctant heroine of a real gem among Scottish songs, decided to ignore him. Burns, in a tone of measured sarcasm, later wrote: "She was too fine a lady *to notice* so plain a compliment." As for Wilhelmina, she lived to the ripe old age of eighty-nine, clutching among her most treasured possessions the letter and song from an audacious tenant farmer, who had immortalized her as: *The Lass o' Ballochmyle.*

Two days after the letter was dispatched to Ballochmyle, Burns sent John Ballantine, a banker in Ayr, and later provost of the town, a copy of a recently composed poem, *A Winter Night.* He informed Ballantine that it was his "first attempt in that irregular kind of measure in which many of our finest Odes are wrote." A section of this poem often quoted to show the poet's radical politics reads:

> See stern Oppression's iron grip,
>   Or mad Ambition's gory hand,
> Sending like blood-hounds from the slip,
>   Woe, Want, and Murder o'er a land!
> Ev'n in the peaceful rural vale,
> Truth, weepin, tells a mournful tale,
> How pamper'd Luxury, Flatt'ry by her side,
> The parasite empoisoning her ear,
> With all the servile wretches in the rear,
> Looks o'er proud Property, extended wide;
> And eyes the simple rustic Hind,
>   Whose toil upholds the glitt'ring show,
> A creature of another kind,
>   Some coarser substance unrefin'd,
> Plac'd for her lordly use thus far, thus vile, below![7]

On the same day, obviously in buoyant spirits, he wrote a letter of rollicking humour jointly addressed to William Chalmers, a lawyer in Ayr, and John McAdam, landowner and agricultural improver. It was Chalmers who had drawn up the deed of assignment transferring the poet's assets to Gilbert. Chalmers had requested of Burns to write some verses for a young lady he was courting - his Dulcinea - as Burns styled her.[8] The poem opening: "Wi' braw new branks in mickle pride" was the outcome. McAdam, as previously mentioned, was the feu superior of Lochlie, involved in the litigation between the poet's father and McClure. In the letter to them Burns declared himself as the: "Poet-Laureat, and Bard in Chief, in and over the Districts and Countries of Kyle, Cunningham and Carrick" - Chalmers and McAdam he regaled as "Students and Practitioners in the ancient and mysterious Science of Confounding Right and Wrong." He had enclosed a bawdy song, probably one of his own, and countinuing in his witty stride made the suggestion:

> We have discovered a certain (bawdy), nefarious, abominable and wicked Song or Ballad, a copy whereof We have here inclosed; Our Will therefore is, that Ye pitch upon and appoint the most execrable Individual of that most execrable Species, known by the appelation, phrase, and nickname of "the Deil's Yell Nowte:" and after having caused him to kindle a fire at the Cross of Ayr, ye shall, at noontide of the day, put into the said wretch's merciless hands the said copy of the said nefarious and wicked Song, to be consumed by fire in the presence of all Beholders, in abhorrence of, and terrorem to, all such Compositions and Composers.[9]

One week later, on Monday 27 November, 1786, the "Poet-Laureat of the Ayrshire Countries" mounted a pony borrowed from George Reid, a farmer at Barquharrie, nearby Ochiltree, and for the first time rode beyond the boundaries of his native shire; his course was set for the Capital, and the sixty mile journey would take him two days. His overnight stop was at Covington Mains where, on arrangements made by Reid, he gratefully accepted the hospitality at the farmhouse of Archibald Prentice. George Reid, incidentally, was the husband of Agnes Tennant, a daughter of the farmer of Glenconner. Burns continued his journey next day and finally arrived in Edinburgh, where his old Mauchline cronie Richmond, agreed to share his room with him, at Baxter's Close, Lawnmarket; the following day he spent in bed - indisposed - suspicions of a hangover cannot be entirely ruled out!

CHAPTER NINE

Scotia's Darling Seat

EDINA! *Scotia's* darling seat!
All hail thy palaces and tow'rs,
Where once beneath a Monarch's feet,
Sat Legislation's sov'reign pow'rs!

Address To Edinburgh

(Burns) looked back on his venture as a "hare-brained ramble,"
and on Edinburgh Society as a "Greenland bay of Indifference."
From the beginning he had recognised that for this small group
of "Patricians" who saw too much of each other, he was merely
a welcome novelty.

Robert Burns: The Man And The Poet
By, Robert Fitzhugh

The early Edinburgh days were spent in making useful contacts, the first of importance being Sir John Whitefoord, who had owned the Ballochmyle estate until financial difficulties had compelled him to sell-out to the Alexanders. He had been the Master of the Masonic Lodge in Tarbolton, where Burns had been initiated into the Craft, and he had now retired to the Capital. Burns next met James Dalrymple of Orangefield, contacted by the way of Ballantine the banker in Ayr, who had been instrumental in encouraging the poet to try for an Edinburgh Edition of his works. Burns repaid the favours shown by Ballantine, by dedicating the poem *The Brigs of Ayr* to the banker. Dalrymple, a nephew of the Revd. William Dalrymple who had baptized Burns in 1759, was a cousin to Lord Glencairn, the Whig aristocrat, whose influence proved vital in getting the *Edinburgh Edition* under way.

It was probably Dalrymple who invited Burns to attend a meeting of the foremost Masonic lodge in the city, Canongate Kilwinning, on the 7 December; at a later meeting on 1 February 1787, he was declared an "assumed member" of this lodge. There is some confusion as to whether or not Burns was actually installed as Poet Laureate of the Lodge. In the "History of the Lodge of Edinburgh", David Murray Lyon declared that: "Burns was never elected to, and never held the office of Poet-Laureate of the Lodge".[1]

The Right Worshipful Master of the lodge was Alexander Fergusson of Craigdarroch, son of the celebrated *Annie Laurie,* he later figured as the drinking 'hero' of Burns's ballad *The Whistle.* The Senior Warden of Canongate Kilwinning was William Dunbar, the "Rattlin, roarin Willie' in the song of that title; William Cruikshank, at whose house Burns lodged for a time, was also a member - his young daughter immortalized as the poet's, *Rosebud By My Early Walk,* and also in the verses beginning: *Beauteous rose-bud, young and gay.* A third William was also a lodge member, William Nicol, for whom Burns later named one of his sons. He was a Latin master at the High School of Edinburgh, a colleague of Cruikshank, who was employed there as a classics master. All three were members of the Crochallan Fencibles, one of several prominent drinking clubs that flourished in the city, and inevitably, Burns was enlisted into the corps.

Another aspect of his social life in Edinburgh centred around what has been termed polite society. He was a guest at the home of the Earl of Glencairn, who appears to have introduced him to the publisher William Creech; Glencairn also secured for him the promise of subscriptions for 100 copies of his proposed new edition, from the membership of the Caledonian Hunt. Professor Dugald Stewart continued his friendship established when Burns dined at Catrine House; he brought the *Kilmarnock Edition* to the attention of Henry Mackenzie who published a review of it in *The Lounger.* The vivacious extrovert, the Duchess of Gordon, entertained him at dinners and balls; she was the darling of the London Tories, and she raved so much about the Ayrshire poet, that whiffs of scandal were heard in the drawing rooms and drinking dens of the rich, in the English capital. Dr Robert Anderson an eminent literary figure, met him and argued politics with him. Anderson professed to be a Whig, and supporter of Fox; he claimed that Burns was a Pittite Tory, and fanatical Jacobite.[2] It must, of course, be remembered that Burns enjoyed nothing more than a good argument and was not adverse to taking the opposite side for the hell of it. Yet, there is indeed evidence of Jacobite sympathies being much to the fore during those Edinburgh days. A description of the poet's personal appearance has been recorded by Anderson:

His person, though neither robust nor elegant, was manly and pleasing; and his countenance, though dark and coarse, uncommonly expressive and interesting. With an air of keen penetration and calm thoughtfulness approaching to melancholy, the usual attendant on genius, there was a kind of stern pride and supercilious elevation about him not incompatible with openness and affability, which might perhaps be properly termed a strong consciousness of intellectual excellence.[3]

Towards the end of February, 1787, the first 300 pages of his new volume had been set in print; this became known as the "stinking edition" due to the famous misprint in the final stanza of: *Address to a Haggis,* which read - "Auld Scotland wants nae stinking ware", later, of course, corrected to "skinking" which glosses as, a thin liquid:

> Ye Pow'rs wha mak mankind your care,
> And dish them out their bill o' fare,
> Auld Scotland wants nae skinking ware
>   That jaups in luggies;   (splashes in its soupdish)
> But, if ye wish her gratefu' pray'r,
>   Gie her a *Haggis!* [4]

In a letter to Mrs Dunlop on the 22 March, 1787, Burns stated that he had "both a second and third Edition going on as the second was begun with too small a number of copies" - the whole totalled 3,000 printed books. The book appeared on 17 April, priced five shillings (25 newpence) to subscribers, six shillings to all others. Creech agreed only to its publication, all other responsibilities for it rested with Burns, who became actively involved in its distribution to save the commission to booksellers. In the following week the poet sold his copyright of the work to publisher Creech for the sum of 100 guineas. He finally got around to paying Burns the sum due on 30 May, 1788, and it was not until February, 1789, that Burns, after much pleading and threatening, at last received his full payment from Creech. The poet informed Mrs Dunlop that he had cleared around £440-£450, and added:

> To keep my brother from ruin, and scattering my aged parent & three sisters comfortless in the world, I advanced him about £200 of that money; this you know was an indispensable affair, as their wellbeing is certainly to me the same as my own.[5]

The relationship between Burns and Creech had begun in amicable enough fashion. When Creech had temporarily left Edinburgh on a business trip to London, in May 1787, Burns took the opportunity of spilling forth some light-hearted stanzas - among them:

O Willie was a witty wight,	(fellow)
And had o' things an unco slight;	(vast knowledge)
Auld Reekie ay he keepit tight,	(Edinburgh)
And trig and braw:	(fine and handsome)
But now they'll busk her like a fright,	(dress)
Willie's awa.-	

The brethren o' the commerce-chaumer	(chamber)
May mourn their loss wi' doolfu' clamour:	(doleful)
He was a dictionar and grammar	
Amang them a':	
I fear they'll now mak mony a stammer,	
Willie's awa.-	

Nae mair we see his levee door	(no more)
Philosophers and Poets pour,	
And toothly critics by the score	
In bloody raw;	
The Adjutant of a' the core	
Willie's awa.-[6]	

Creech's 'levee door' alluded to the custom of several literary figures, Burns now being one of them, who gathered at the publisher's house at breakfast time. Creech remained a bachelor throughout his life, and at one stage, much to his embarrassment and fury, he was romantically linked, in a London Journal, with the well known prostitute Margaret Mathews, who adopted the name Burns, and earned some recognition from her famous namesake:

CEASE, ye prudes, your envious railing,
    Lovely Burns has charms - *confess;*
True it is, she had one failing,
    Had ae woman ever less?[7]

The actual printing of the *Edinburgh Edition* was the task of Creech's partner, William Smellie, a man with an extensive range of literary awareness, he had edited, and written many entries in the first issue of *Encyclopaedia Britannica*. It is generally accepted that it was Smellie who

had founded the Crochallan Fencibles, and brought Burns into their ranks -
the poet depicted him thus:

> (Shrew'd Willie Smellie to) Crochallan came;
> The old cock'd hat, the brown surtout, the same;
> His grisly beard just bristling in its might,
> 'Twas four long nights and days from shaving-night;
> His uncomb'd, hoary locks, wild-staring thatch'd,
> A head for thought profound and clear unmatch'd:
> Yet, tho' his caustic wit was biting rude,
> His heart was warm, benevolent and good.[8]

During those early days in Edinburgh Burns made his pilgrimage to
the grave of Robert Fergusson, his predecessor in the Scottish Muse, and he
was dismayed to find it unmarked and dilapidated. He resolved to amend
matters by having an inscribed stone erected, the cost of which he was more
than willing to meet. The inscription gave Fergusson's birth year as 1751;
it should have read 1750, no matter, the idea in itself was sound enough. He
gave a copy of Fergusson's poems to a young poetess, Rebekah
Carmichael, and another copy to the wife of Andrew Dalziel, professor of
Greek at Edinburgh University. In a letter to a friend, dated 25 January
1787, (Robert's 28th birthday) Dalziel commented on this poet who had
lately arrived in town:

> He is a fellow of strong common sense, and by his own industry
> has read a good deal of English, both prose and verse.....He
> runs the risk, however, of being spoiled by the excessive
> attention paid him just now by persons of all ranks. Those who
> know him best, say he has too much good sense to allow
> himself to be spoiled.

By the springtime of his first year in the city Burns had agreed to take
a tour of the Borders, in the company of a young trainee lawyer, Robert
Ainslie, to whom Burns could "talk nonsense without forfeiting some
degree of esteem." They rode out of Edinburgh on Saturday 5 May, and
reached the home of Ainslie's family in Dunse, by evening. In the journal
recorded by Burns, mention is made of visiting, Kelso, Coldstream,
Roxburgh, Jedburgh, Melrose, Selkirk, and several other places; at St Abb's
he and Ainslie were initiated as Royal Arch freemasons. After Ainslie
returned to Edinburgh the poet continued his trip o'er the border into the

English town of Carlisle. The border scenery he found attractive - likewise some of the poeple; Rachel Ainslie was described as "an angel" - Miss Isabella Lindsay, a positive delight, had brought him "within a point and a half of being damnably in love."

He arrived in Dumfries to be presented with the freedom of the burgh; he was also presented with a letter informing him that a certain May Cameron, on whose behalf it was written, was "in trouble" and wondering what she could do; so he taxed Ainslie's friendship far enough to request that he should call upon the unfortunate May and give her ten or twelve shillings. When she swore out a writ against him for the support of her child, Burns acknowledged it and paid. From Dumfries Burns set his course for Mauchline, and on the 8 June, 1787, Caledonia's celebrated bard made his *eclatant* return to his former hometown. Letters were dispatched: one to James Smith, who had left Mauchline for Linlithgow in the previous year, the other to Willie Nicol, his drinking crony in Edinburgh; both being informed about his singular regard for his favourite hero: "that great Personage, Satan" - discovered in the pages of his pocket Milton. At the end of the month he decided to tour the West Highlands going as far as Inverary, where he complained bitterly about a lack of welcome:

> WHOE'ER he be that sojourns here,
> I pity much his case,
> Unless he come to wait upon
> The Lord their God, his Grace[9]   (Duke of Argyll)

There is every likelihood that he called at Greenock's Old West Kirk cemetery at the outset of this tour to pay his respects at the grave of his dead love, Mary Campbell. Her mother made it known that he had made an approach asking for a keepsake of the Highland lassie, but she had refused his request. Mary's father, for whatever reason, detested the very name of Burns till death itself closed his bitterness in the year 1815. Her brother Robert also appears to have remained hostile, though her younger sister, Annie Campbell, who later named her own daughter Mary, after her celebrated aunt, carried no ill-will towards Burns, and the youngest of the Campbells, Archibald, is said to have given a presentation copy of the poet's works to the Burns Club in Greenock.

On the 2 August, 1787, whilst still at Mauchline, he wrote his long autobiographical letter to John Moore, which was "unluckily forgot among other papers at Glasgow" - it was finally sent from Edinburgh on 23 September 1787. Moore was a political liberal whose friendships during his period in France, included Thomas Paine and the Earl of Lauderdale, who were frequent dining companions. His secretary and amanuensis, for a time, was the fiery revolutionary, Helen Maria Williams, who had written to Burns highly praising his verses on the "Mountain Daisy". Burns's contact with Dr Moore had stemmed from Mrs Dunlop who, being acquainted with the doctor, had sent him a copy of the *Kilmarnock Edition,* and he, in turn, had asked her to get Burns to write to him. An interesting aside to the famous letter is found in the comments made by Burns on discovering a transcript copy of it:

> Know all whom it may concern, that I, the Author, am not answerable for the false spelling & injudicious punctuation in the foregoing transcript of my letter to Dr Moore.- I have something generous in my temper that cannot bear to see or hear the Absent wronged, & I am very much hurt to observe that in several instances the transcriber has injured & mangled the proper name & principal title of a Personage of the very first distinction in all that is valuable among men, Antiquity, abilities & power; (Virtue every body knows is an obsolete business) I mean, the Devil.- Considering that the Transcriber was one of the Clergy, an order that owe the very bread they eat to the said Personage's exertions, the affair was absolutely unpardonable.; R.B.- [10]

On the 25 August, Burns set out from Edinburgh on a tour of the Highlands, in the company of Willie Nicol; he informed Ainslie that the journey would be in a chaise: "Nicol thinks it more comfortable than horseback, to which I say, Amen." In twenty-two days the pair covered almost 600 miles; saw many interesting places, and met several notable people, among them, Robert Graham of Fintry, who would prove to be a stalwart friend of the poet's. The meeting with Graham, a Commissioner of the Excise, took place at Blair Castle, home of the Duke of Atholl. Nicol's notorious temper, and general impatience proved irksome to Burns, but at least their friendship did survive the journey. At their first stop, in Stirling, Burns inscribed the lines of Jacobite sentiment on the window pane of an inn, with his diamond stylus, a present from Lord Glencairn. The closing sentiments of brutal truth directed against the royal family, were hardly diplomatic from one who was, by now, seeking, employment as a government agent in the Excise:

> The injur'd STEWART line are gone,
> A Race outlandish fills their throne:
> An idiot race, to honor lost;
> Who know them best despise them most.-[11]

A call was made at Gordon Castle, and Burns would have liked to spend some time there; however, Nicol's surly mood once more took precedence and propelled them on their way, earning him a measure of wrath for posterity from his poetic friend:

> May that obstinate son of Latin prose be curst to Scotch-mile periods; while Declension & Conjugation, Gender, Number, and Time, under the ragged banners of Dissonance and disarrangement eternally rank against him in hostile array. [12]

On their way south by the east coast route, Burns was able to meet relations of his father's at Stonehaven. On the 16 September, as the poet's journal relates, came the end of the Highland tour: "Come through a cold barren Country to Queensferry - dine - cross the Ferry, and come to Edinburgh."

CHAPTER TEN

Beneath The Ochil Hills

WHERE braving angry Winter's storms
The lofty Ochels rise,
Far in their shade, my Peggy's charms
First blest my wandering eyes.-

Where Braving Angry Winter's Storms

I would give my best song to my worst enemy, I mean the merit
of making it, to have you and Charlotte by me. You are angelic
creatures, and would pour oil and wine into my wounded spirit.
.....The "Ochel-hills," you shall probably have next week for
yourself.

Letter to Peggy Chalmers
19 December 1787

By the beginning of October 1787, Burns was again restless in
Edinburgh awaiting on his settlement with Creech. On the 4th of that
month, in the company of Dr James McKittrick Adair, whose friendship the
poet had acquired through the Lawries of Loudon, he set off on a short tour
of Stirlingshire. The focal point would be the Harvieston estate in the valley
of the River Devon, and Burns was hopeful that at Harvieston he would
chance upon Margaret Chalmers, or as he appears to have called her, Peggy.

She was a few years younger than Burns, born at Fingland near
Kirkcudbright; her father, James Chalmers, had sold off his lands in that
area, and had moved to Braehead farm near Mauchline. This has led to
speculation from some sources that Burns may have known her prior to his
stay in Edinburgh. At any rate, he met with her at the home of Dr Blacklock,
where Peggy frequently visited to play the piano and sing for the elderly
blind poet. It has been presumed by most Burns scholars that Peggy was the
recipient of his declaration of love:

I know you will laugh at it, when I tell you that your Piano (forte)
and you together have play'd the deuce somehow, about my
heart. I was once a zealous Devotee to your Sex, but you know
the black story at home. My breast has been widowed these
many months, and I thought myself proof against the fascinating

witchcraft.....I have a miserable bad symptom, (which I doubt threatens ill): when you whisper, or look kindly to another, it gives me a draught of damnation.[1]

The Harvieston estate belonged to an Edinburgh lawyer named John Tait, who had married Peggy's aunt. During an eight day stay, Burns and Adair, appear to have respectively courted Peggy and her cousin Charlotte Hamilton, making several excursions into the beautiful surrounding countryside. That Burns made no exertion on his Muse to cover the scenes seemingly disappointed the others. He did, however, pay poetic compliment to Charlotte with the song, *The Banks of the Devon,* and wrote two songs for Peggy Chalmers, *My Peggy's Charms,* and, *Where Braving Angry Winter's Storms,* the latter being set to the dramatic air, *Neil Gow's Lament for Lord Abercairny:*

> Blest be the wild, sequester'd glade
>   And blest the day and hour,
> Where Peggy's charms I first survey'd,
>   When first I felt their pow'r.-
>
> The tyrant Death with grim controul
>   May seize my fleeting breath,
> But tearing Peggy from my soul
>   Must be a stronger death.- [2]

Burns left no journal of this break in the Devon valley; however, Dr Adair supplied biographical information to James Currie for his four-volume edition of Burns's works published in the year 1800. At Stirling on their way to Harvieston, Burns and he had met with a party of travellers from Edinburgh, among them: "a character in many respects congenial with that of Burns." This was Willie Nicol, and Adair could hardly conceal his amusement in studying the pair:

.....the same wit and power of conversation; the same fondness for convivial society, and thoughtlessness of tomorrow, characterised both; Jacobitical principles in politics were common to both of them, and these have been suspected, since the revolution in France, to have given place in each, to opinions apparently opposite. I regret that I have preserved no *memorabilia* of their conversation, either on this or other occasions when I happened to meet them together.

Adair's courtship of Charlotte Hamilton proved successful; she agreed to marry him, and did so on 16 November 1789. He had Burns to thank for introducing him to the woman who became his wife:

> He introduced me to the family, and there was formed my first acquaintance with Mrs Hamilton's eldest daughter, to whom I have been married for nine years. Thus was I indebted to Burns for a connexion from which I have derived, and expect further to derive, much happiness.

The courtship of Burns was not at all successful. Peggy Chalmers, in her later years, she died in 1843, revealed that Burns had asked her to marry him, but that she had politely declined. They had, however, remained on terms of friendship, and Burns corresponded with her until close to her marriage, on 9 December, 1788, to a banker named Lewis Hay. In his last known letter to her Burns told her that he had "lived more of real life" in the eight days spent with her at Harvieston than he could have in eight years with almost anybody else. Ian McIntyre has pointed out that Burns actually coupled Peggy's sister Cochrane (Lady M'Kenzie) with her in this emotional outburst; the text is rather misleading, but the 'you' must surely revert to the singular, even in mid-sentence, to make sense of his intimacy with Peggy:

> I can truly say that, all the exterior of life apart, I never saw two whose esteem flattered the nobler feelings of my soul - I will not say, more, but, so much as Lady M'Kenzie and Miss Chalmers. When I think of you - hearts the best, minds the noblest, of human kind - unfortunate, even in the shades of life - when I think I have met with you, and have lived more of real life with you in eight days than I can do with almost anybody I meet with in eight years - when I think on the improbability of meeting you in this world again - I could sit down and cry like a child! - [3]

The memory of Peggy Chalmers probably continued to haunt Burns to the end of his days: he admitted that her name was "indelibly written in (his) heart's core" - whilst the very last line of his poetic career carried sentiments for her which seemingly betrayed the yearning he never quite rescinded: "No love but thine my heart shall know.-"

The letters which Burns sent to Peggy were, according to Cromek, thrown into the fire, "in an evil hour", by Charlotte Hamilton. It is presumed that transcripts had already been made of the sections which are now in print; the alternative suggestion that they were constructed from the charred remains seems doubtful. Allan Cunningham, said: "nothing was saved except such fragments as were found among the Bard's memoranda", but Cunningham's reputation for invention must here be taken into consideration. As De Lancey Ferguson noted, several of the fragmentary letters are dated, and Burns rarely dated draft copies.

The letter addressed to, "My Dear Countrywoman", undated, was published by Currie, from a draft found among the poet's papers. It was corrected and completed in *Burns Club Facsimilies, 1908;* the MS is now lodged in the Huntington Library, San Marino, California. Although James Barke claimed that the recipient of this letter "on the available evidence" was more likely to be Christina Laurie (Lawrie), rather than Peggy Chalmers, his reasoning is not at all convincing in its presentation, and suspiciously reflects a novelist's anxiety to gain the story at the expense of the facts.[4]

It is certainly beyond question that Peggy Chalmers was a lady of quite exceptional quality; her entry in the *Burns Encyclopedia* lists her as: "one of the only two really first-class women with whom Burns became friendly" - Maria Riddell being the other. In the aftermath of his unsuccessful wooing of Peggy, a new fascination of feminine charm soon caught Burns's attention: her name was Agnes McLehose, or Nancy, to her intimate friends, but she was soon signing her letters to him as Clarinda! Robin alas, was confronted with a slight obstacle in his path of true love - Clarinda was a married woman!

They first met on 4 December, 1787, at the home of Miss Erskine Nimmo, who, as it so happened, was a close friend of Peggy Chalmers. Nancy's immediate reaction was to invite the poet to tea, an invitation he gratefully accepted. The visit, however, had to be postponed due to the actions of a drunken coachman who caused Burns to fall and sustain a painful knee injury which laid him up. He notified Nancy of his predicament, and received a gracious reply. A flurry of letters soon passed between them. By the 12 December he was informing her: "I swear solemnly...to remember you in all the pride and warmth of friendship until

The Twa Dogs

NEWFOUNDLAND
His hair, his size, his mouth, his lugs,
Show'd he was nane o' Scotland's dogs;
But whalpet some place far abroad,
Whare sailors gang to fish for Cod.

COLLIE
The tither was a *ploughman's collie,*
A rhyming, ranting, raving billie,
Wha for his friend an' comrade had him,
And in his freaks had *Luath* ca'd him....

Burns had taken the opportunity to immortalize old Luath, the family dog at Lochlie farm, in this poem which opened his first book, the *Kilmarnock Edition,* in 1786. Robert later owned a Newfoundland, named Thurlow, during his tenancy at Ellisland. The dog often accompanied him when he rode across the countryside on his Excise business.

Plate 1

MOSSGIEL FARM
(1784-86)

In March 1784 Robert, as the head of his family unit in the aftermath of their father's death, took the tenancy of Mossgiel farm in Mauchline parish. In accordance with the old custom he adopted the farm's name and styled himself as Rob Mossgiel. It was the most productive period of his poetic career. As Robert Louis Stevenson put it, Burns: "attacked literature with a hand that seemed capable of moving mountains", whilst at Mossgiel. During his occupation of this farm he acknowledged his marriage to Jean Armour; however, with neither official registration, nor church blessing, the legality of this irregular marriage has been questioned, and James Armour compelled his daughter to repudiate the Bard of Mossgiel as her husband. Burns and Armour were legally married two years later.

Plate 2

JAMES CUNNINGHAM Fourteenth Earl of Glencairn
(1749-1791)

Robert Burns held no other patron in such high esteem as he did Lord
Glencairn. A son born to the poet in 1794 was named, James Glencairn
Burns, in the earl's honour. The factor of Glencairn's Finlayston estate near
Port-Glasgow, Alexander Dalziel, is said to have drawn the earl's attention
to Burns's *Kilmarnock Edition*. Dalziel, a friend of the poet Fergusson,
became a charter member of the Greenock Burns Club. The Earl of
Glencairn died, on a voyage home from Portugal, on 30 January, 1791, and
was buried at Falmouth in Cornwall. Sadly, it has been recorded that
Burns's poignant, *Lament for James, Earl of Glencairn*, was not even
acknowledged by the Cunningham family.

Plate 3

DR JOHN MOORE
(1729-1802)

Born at Stirling, and educated at Glasgow Grammar School, and University, Moore was apprenticed to John Gordon, the surgical instructor to Smollett. He was the favoured recipient of Burns's autobiographical letter in 1787. Moore's friendship with Paine and Lauderdale, and his employment of Helen Maria Williams as his amanuensis, placed him in the liberal camp in politics; Burns was, therefore, disappointed at "the honest Doctor's whining" over the executions of the French King and Queen. It should, however, be noted that Thomas Paine himself went to considerable lengths, and at risk to his own safety, to prevent the King's "deserved fate" on the scaffold.

Plate 4

AGNES McLEHOSE
(1758-1841)
Clarinda

Nancy, as she was known, first met Robert Burns at the home of Miss Erskine Nimmo, in Alison Square Edinburgh, on 4 December, 1787. An epistolary courtship developed in which they decided to take Arcadian names. Nancy called the poet Sylvander - man of the woods - the name Clarinda, a derivative of Clare, was used by Edmund Spenser in his epic work, *The Faerie Queene,* (1596) and had an appeal to poetic fashion in the 17th century. Burns claimed that one of his favourite toasts was, *To Mrs Mack,* and even after his marriage to Jean Armour, he renewed his friendship with Nancy McLehose.

Plate 5

THE POET'S LAST HOUSE

On the 10 September, 1791, Robert Burns renounced his lease on Ellisland farm, and by November had arranged to move his family into a town dwelling in Dumfries. His career in the land was now finally over, and his future lay in his employment as an exciseman. The house which they rented stood in the Wee Vennel (now Bank Street), in those days, not a particularly pleasant site. On 19 May, 1793, the Burns family moved to the Millbrae Vennel (now Burns Street), the final home of the poet - in this house he died in the early hours of the morning, on 21 July, 1796.

Plate 6

- I cease to be! To-morrow, and every day, till I see you, you shall hear from me."

Only one letter from Burns for the period 13 to 27 December has survived; it has been given the conjectural date 20 December, by interpolation. The use of Arcadian names was soon agreed. A letter from Nancy to Robert, dated 20 December, informed him that she would address him as Sylvander (a character in an *entertaining amour* published twenty years previously) whilst she, for the first time, signed herself Clarinda. In his letter of 28 December Burns commented: "I like the idea of Arcadian names." In the same letter he begged her pardon for a fragment scrawl sent the previous day - this scrawl has not survived! The text of Nancy's letter of 20 December 1787, however, relies solely on a transcript made by Sir Samuel Egerton Brydges from whose collection it was apparently taken. According to J C Ewing, the text has obviously been tampered with in the process of constructing the revised, and only version, now available.[5]

As the relationship developed Clarinda became ever more aware of her marital status, expressing her anxiety to keep matters on to a purely Platonic basis. Her conscience was guided by her Calvinist beliefs and concerns about the prying eyes of the Kirk. Her worthless husband had wilfully abandoned her, but although he was now a debauched rake in far off Jamaica, she was still legally tied to him, and flirting with a poet who already carried a dangerous reputation was a matter not to be taken lightly. When her snooping clergyman, the Revd. Kemp - splendidly described by James Mackay as, "a sanctimonious lecher" - brought a reproof to Clarinda, she passed the details on to Burns who exploded in wrath:

> I have not patience to read the Puritanical scrawl. Damned sophistry! Ye heavens, thou God of nature, thou Redeemer of mankind! ye look down with approving eyes on a passion inspired by the purest flame, and guarded by truth, delicacy, and honor; but the half-inch soul of an unfeeling, cold-blooded, pitiful Presbyterian bigot cannot forgive anything above his dungeon-bosom and foggy head.[6]

He sent off this letter on Wednesday, 13 February, 1788, opening it by addressing her as, *My ever dearest Clarinda,* and followed it up with a further epistle carrying the same date, and stating it to be written at

Midnight. This merely opened with a rather curt, *Madam,* and informed her that he had suffered a wretched day. He was now preparing for a sleepless night, but he had taken the time after all, to read the "Puritanical scrawl" which he proceeded to describe as a "haughty dictatorial letter". He advised her to pay no heed to it - she was answerable only to God, and not to any interfering fellow-creature, whose arrogance had intruded her private affairs.

The correspondence from Burns to Clarinda has stretched to over fifty surviving epistles, the final one from him dated in late June 1794. The name Clarinda, if the text of the Brydges transcript can be relied upon, would seem to have been Nancy's idea. Yet, it does seem strange that Burns made very little of this beyond a casual comment, and inevitably leads to the view that he may have guided her to this pseudonym in a non-surviving letter. Nancy herself, in the aftermath of Burns's death, thought she had signed herself Clitander, though whether she made a genuine mistake, or was being deliberately devious, is now certainly open to question. J C Ewing noted that Clarinda, "had been a favourite name with writers since the days of Edmund Spenser"; to be more precise, Spenser himself had used the name in his lengthy poem, *The Faerie Queene,* in the fifth book, cantata five.[7]

The name, poetically, can be traced to Clorinda, the tragic figure in the epic poem of Torquato Tasso, (*Jerusalem Liberated*) produced in 1581, who was accidently killed by her lover, Tancred. Spenser leaned heavily on *Jerusalem Liberated,* as a model, when he composed his own masterpiece, *The Faerie Queene,* the first three books of which were published in 1590, the remainder in 1596, the name Clarinda possibly prompted by Tasso's heroine. Burns had first read Tasso in a copy borrowed from Mrs. Dunlop, which he commented on in two letters to her in the spring of 1788. As for the affair with his Clarinda, it has been adequately summed up by John De Lancey Ferguson:

> Despite most of the biographers, the affair cannot be dignified into a tragedy. It is, rather an ironic comedy - a full-length study of the mess into which two sentimentalists with a gift for words can get themselves.[8]

Even after Burns's marriage to Jean Armour in April 1788,

denounced by Clarinda as Sylvander's "perfidious treachery', their relationship did not come to a complete end. Her anger had sufficiently cooled by 1790 that she took the initiative to reopen the correspondence. In December 1791, Burns spent a full week in Edinburgh, and took it upon himself to meet her several times. Their final parting has been recorded in the lyrics of two exceptional love-songs, *Gloomy December,* and the better known, *Ae Fond Kiss:*

> Ae fond kiss, and then we sever!
> Ae fareweel, Alas, for ever!
> Deep in heart-wrung tears I'll pledge thee,
> Warring sighs and groans I'll wage thee.- [9]

In the early weeks of 1788 Burns had decided that his stay in Edinburgh must come to an end. He was once again facing the old problem of how to organize his future security; the Excise drew his attention, despite its obvious shortcomings, as a means of steady employment with a regular, though hardly enhancing, salary. Several patrons cautioned him here and advised on a return to farming. To this end he followed up a deal proposed to him by Patrick Miller who had, in 1785, purchased the Dalswinton estate on the banks of the River Nith in Dumfriesshire. Miller's offer to the poet was Ellisland farm on a seventy-six year lease, at a rent of fifty pounds per annum, rising after three years to seventy pounds, with an advance of £300 from Miller to cover the costs of building a farmhouse and making other general improvements. From his first look at the ground Burns was sceptical, the soil looked completely exhausted; time and money in considerable amounts would be required to get it into working order, and he was well aware of Gilbert's current hardships at Mossgiel. He played Miller along for quite some time, not at all anxious to commit himself. In the end he decided to consult John Tennant of Glenconner: "A worthy, intelligent farmer, my father's friend and my own", as he described the man he hailed in verse as: "The ace an' wale of honest men". To Burns's surprise Glenconner, on travelling down to look over Ellisland, was quite enthusiastic about the venture. This opinion, coupled with the location of the farm itself, probably swayed Burns. To a poet who liked nothing better than to tempt his Muse whilst rambling along the banks of a pleasant stream, Ellisland farm was truly a heavenly setting.

The events in his life were once more gathering pace. Having more or less made up his mind on a return to farming he also decided to ensure some protection for his future by pursuing a career in the Excise. Friends in high places were sought and their assistance solicited. This included sorting out his little indiscretion when he had publicly branded the royal family as "an idiot race" - he had, however, broken the window pane which had carried the offending lines, though it had not saved him from being taken behind closed doors, where, much to his considerable annoyance, he had to endure being "lectured like a schoolboy". To the insulted King, he was now obliged to take an oath of allegiance! He was also conscious of the social opprobrium the job carried - at a salary of £50 per annum, and a measure of security, he wondered if it was all worthwhile.

Complications seemed to come to Robin in multiple numbers; in the midst of sorting out his future came news from Mauchline that Jean Armour, as the result of his dallying with her during his *eclatant* return to the parish in June, 1787, was again pregnant. On the 3 March 1788, Armour gave birth to twin girls; barely a week before this event, Burns had informed Clarinda:

> Now for a little news that will please you.- I, this morning as I came home, called for a certain woman.- I am disgusted with her; I cannot endure her! I, while my heart smote me for the profanity, tried to compare her with my Clarinda: 'twas setting the expiring glimmer of a farthing taper beside the cloudless glory of the meridian sun. Here was tasteless insipidity, vulgarity of soul, and mercenary fawning; there polished good sense, heaven-born genius, and the most generous, the most delicate, the most tender Passion.- I have done with her and she with me.- [10]

Within a few weeks of writing this, Robert Burns was confidentially informing his close friend James Smith that he had taken the "certain woman" of the Clarinda letter (Jean Armour), as his wife. Both twins died; one on 10 March, the second death occurring twelve days later. James Mackay has suggested that the twins were not born on 3 March at all, but several days after that date. This is an attempt to take some heat out of the notorious 'horse-litter' incident, described in an unsavoury bragging letter which Burns allegedly wrote to Robert Ainslie, *circa* 3 March - the MS has never been traced. The text appeared in the *Merry Muses* edition of 1872 (erroneously dated 1827); it had already been given, in part, by Allan

Cunningham in 1834. Reference has been made to an indecent letter from Burns to Ainslie supposedly having been destroyed by an Edinburgh bookseller named Stillie.

Franklyn Bliss Snyder in his biography of Burns stated that Burns himself entered the date 3 March 1788 in the family Bible, and Snyder, drawing his information from the Burial Register for Mauchline Parish, verified the deaths: "two laconic entries, which bring the brief stories of these unnamed children to a somewhat pathetic close", as 10th and 22 March respectively. This refutes Mackay's claim that no previous writer bothered to consult the Register, and also his added claim that the birth date of 3 March relied on Jean Armour's own reminiscences given in the year 1825. In somewhat pensive vein, Richard Fowler ruefully reflected that:

> When the bardolaters make their move to have Robert of Mossgiel canonized, the events of a few weeks early in 1788 will make the task of the *advocatus diaboli* a very brief one.[11]

During March and April of that year Burns underwent a course of training and instruction, at Mauchline and Tarbolton, in preparation for a career in the Excise. On the 28 April an Excise Commission was issued to him:

> SEARCHING auld wives' barrells,
>   Ochon, the day!
> That clarty barm should stain my laurels;   (dirty yeast)
>   But - what'll ye say!
> These muvin' things ca'd wives and weans   (moving) (children)
> Wad muve the very hearts o' stanes! [12]

The responsibilites which now loomed before him as a family man in his marriage to Jean, and his anxiety to set up home at Ellisland with her and his young son, Robbie, had seemingly persuaded him that an Excise appointment was an important move to safeguard their collective future. The erstwhile rebel was now about to become the hired servant of King and Country, bound by his oath of fealty! - or so it appeared!

CHAPTER ELEVEN

Land of God's Riddings

Burns declared, after a shower had fallen on a field of new-sown and new-rolled barley, that it looked like a new paved street! "Soil, said he.....there never was such soil; but I see how it has been - God has riddled the hale creation, and flung the riddings on Ellisland!"

Allan Cunningham

The precise details, circumstances, and exact date of Burns's second marriage to Jean Armour, are not known. A letter to James Smith dated, 28 April, 1788, is the earliest recorded reference to him taking Jean Armour as his wife, though a letter to Peggy Chalmers three weeks earlier hinted at his situation. He also apparently mentioned her as Mrs Burns at Gavin Hamilton's breakfast table, in the presence of Robert Aiken, but no date of this incident has been preserved. The traditional belief around Mauchline was that Hamilton himself, being a Justice of the Peace, married them in his writing study. Another source states that one, John Farquhar-Gray, laird of Gilmilnscroft, an estate in Sorn, carried out the ceremony.[1]

When Burns later approached the Kirk in a bid to have its blessings on the marriage some complications arose. The Revd. William Auld wanted proof of an irregular marriage between Burns and Armour, for which the poet assured him that a fine had been paid to a Justice of the Peace. This "irregular marriage" can only really refer to the affair of 1786, and the lines given by Burns to Armour, which were subsequently mutilated by lawyer Aiken. An interesting point has been made by Hugh Douglas (*The Tinder Heart,* 1966) that, in 1788, Burns and Armour did not go through with a wedding ceremony as such, but rather affirmed their previous vows of 1786. Snyder thought that Burns, under pressure from Auld to supply the marital details, "invented a pious fiction." Burns, it is true, could be impetuous, bold, even rash on occasions, but he was never a complete fool. Mauchline was a small tight-knit community, and like any other place, full of gossiping about any given scandal - Burns would have invented no "pious fiction" being well aware that the holy beagles would soon ferret out the truth of the matter. He was far too astute to leave himself exposed to the consequences of the Kirk uncovering him treading an avenue of lies and deceit.

Thus, when Burns sought from his old crony James Smith the favour of written confirmation that an irregular marriage had indeed taken place in 1786, he certainly was not attempting to persuade Smith to commit perjury, as James Mackay has suggested. Smith was perfectly capable of verifying as a witness, within the bounds of law and personal integrity, that Robert Burns had given Jean Armour the marriage lines of 1786. Since Auld had issued Burns with a Certificate of Bachelorhood, in the aftermath of the 1786 affair, he would have wanted to be fully aware of all the past circumstances. The Kirk finally consented to acknowledge them as husband and wife on 5 August, 1788.

The reasons why he chose to marry Jean Armour, and of the sudden turning away from Clarinda at the very pinnacle of his raging passions for her, have prompted many comments. Robert Louis Stevenson declared that: "A more astonishing stage-trick is not to be found." The novelist waxed sarcastically over the attributes placed by Burns on his new wife, which included a good singing voice capable of "rising with ease to a B natural":-

> Let her manage a farm with sense, let her voice rise to B natural all day long, she would still be a peasant to her lettered lord, an object of pity rather than of equal affection.....From the outset it was a marriage that had no root in nature; and we find him, ere long, lyrically regretting Highland Mary, renewing correspondence with Clarinda in the warmest language, on doubtful terms with Mrs Riddel, and on terms unfortunately beyond any question with Anne Park.[2]

As for Clarinda, according to Robert Chambers, she had the contempt for Jean Armour "that is often entertained by a woman of superficial culture for a woman who can lay no claim to culture at all." Not unnaturally, Clarinda maintained to her dying day that Burns's marriage "was a fatal mistake." Jean Armour's biographer, Peter Westwood, has made it clear that she met Clarinda during a visit made to Edinburgh, in the aftermath of Burns's death.[3]

The summer of 1788 found Burns spending his time in equal spells at

Ellisland, which lay within the parish of Dunscore, and at Mauchline. He told his Edinburgh friend Alexander Cunningham, in a letter written at the end of July, that he spent some eight or ten days alternatively at both places. He eventually settled into "a hovel.....pervious to every blast", less than one mile down river from the farm. He lamented that he only escaped being chilled to death by being nearly suffocated with the smoke. The poem addressed to Hugh Parker vividly described his plight:

> Here, ambush'd by the chimla cheek,   (fireside)
> Hid in an atmosphere of reek,
> I hear a wheel thrum i' the neuk,   (spinning-wheel noise
> I hear it - for in vain I leuk: (look)   in the corner)
> The red peat gleams the fiery kernal,
> Enhusked by a fog infernal:
> Here, for my wonted rhyming raptures,
> I sit and count my sins by chapters;
> For life and spunk like ither Christians,
> I'm dwindled down to mere existence;
> Wi' nae converse but Gallowa' bodies,
> Wi' nae kend face but Jenny Geddes.[4]   (no known) (his mare)

The hovel lay under the shadow of an ivy-covered keep, named the Isle, which dated back to the days of the Red Comyn. The outgoing tenants, the Cullies, were deeply religious, and had heard from local sources that the newcomer was a freethinker who scoffed at scriptures. However, they appear to have treated Burns with reasonable civility; when Mrs Cullie ventured the subject of religion with him, Burns astonished her with his knowledge of the Bible - she informed her husband that the man (Burns) "kenned mair about the guid book than the very minister himself."

The "hovel" was obviously no fit place to bring his wife and surviving child Robbie, now almost two years old. As he surveyed the slow progress on the farmhouse at Ellisland which would serve as their new home, Burns appears to have been lonely and unhappy with his lot. It was undoubtedly during this period that he composed the best song he would ever write for Jean - *Of a' the Airts,* and, quite possibly around the same time, *O Were I on Parnassus Hill.* In all, fourteen songs have been attributed to the charms of Jean; but some may be questioned as her's: *And Maun I Still on Menie Doat* - with its pitifully weak chorus was thought, by Scott Douglas, to allude to Jean Armour because of its reference to jet-black eyes: the conjecture being that when estranged from Armour he had substituted Menie for Jeanie - would he not have restored her name when they came together again? "The chorus", declared Burns, "was composed by a gentleman in Edinburgh, a particular friend of the Author's." The general opinion is that he composed it himself. James Mackay states that the chorus is ancient, but offers no authority for this averment. The superb song, *Their Groves O Sweet Myrtle,* is frequently credited to Armour; however, it was written at a time when Burns was enchanted by Chloris, and the Jean of these verses is, therefore, much more likely to be Lorimer rather than Armour.

By the end of 1788 Jean Armour had moved to Nithsdale, joining her husband in rented accommodation, Robbie continued to live with the Burns family at Mossgiel until well into the following year. Burns had, in the meantime, made the acquaintance of a neighbouring couple in his new environment, Captain Robert Riddell of Glenriddell and his wife Elizabeth; soon the poet was on terms of the closest friendship with them. Riddell was a most accomplished fellow; he had been educated at the Universities of St Andrews and Edinburgh, before embarking on a military career which took him to the rank of captain in 1771. He retired early from the services and had settled into the estate left to him by his father. He sold Glenriddell, but kept the family home at Friars' Carse where Robert Burns became a frequent, and most welcome visitor. Riddell's interests included the study of local archaeology, and he contributed articles to newspapers and journals on this subject and others; he was a member of the London Society of Antiquaries - of special appeal to Burns was the fact that his new-found friend was a talented musician who was perfectly capable of composing airs for Scottish songs. Indeed, in the fullness of time he supplied the music for several of Burns's songs, including: *The Whistle; Nithsdale's Welcome Home; The Blue-Eyed Lassie,* and *The Day Returns.* The poet would also find common ground with Riddell's liberal and democratic politics. In April of that year Burns and Riddell agreed to found a country library system which they named, the Monkland Friendly Society - the poet informed Peter Hill the bookseller in Edinburgh:

> Capt. R- gave his infant society a great many of his old books, else I had written you on that subject; but one of these days I shall trouble you with a Commission for "the Monkland friendly Society"- a copy of the Spectator, Mirror & Lounger, Man of

The 'religious pieces' which the members themselves selected, he subsequently described as "damned trash". Capt. Riddell was elected President of the society, and his valued name in the locality ensured a secure patronage; however, as Ian McIntyre noted, it was the enthusiasm and general hard graft of Robert Burns which really promoted the good it undoubtedly did for the community.[6] The poet supplied the entry for Sir John Sinclair's *Statistical Account of Scotland* which gave a description of the rules and costs to each member, pointing out that each could select works of his choice in rotation - he also declared that, those among the lower classes who troubled to raise their education by reading were likely to be "a superior being to (their) neighbour, who, perhaps, stalks beside the team, very little removed, except in shape, from the brutes he drives." He appears to have chanced upon one such neighbour in the latter category "who has made himself absolutely contemptible in my eyes by his silly, garrulous pruriency."

The Ellisland period produced only one major poem, *Tam o' Shanter.* His literary ambitions now centred on songwriting, and also in collecting old songs which he repaired to suit favoured tunes. It was a turning point which later brought the despair of Robert Louis Stevenson who saw in it a move away from producing great literature to merely wasting his precious hours, "whittling cherrystones". Others would disagree; for among the undoubted cherrystones, he also produced quite a collection of exquisite lyric gems. Burns took upon himself the task of supplying his songs for two very different editors, James Johnson, and George Thomson.

Johnson was an engraver and music seller in Edinburgh, and met the poet during his spell in the capital. By that time the engraver had already made some progress on his desire to see Scottish songs presented in books, which he styled as a, *Scots Musical Museum* - his first volume containing one hundred songs, being in the press. He invited Burns to join his project, and with scant regard for the workload he would take on without any payment whatever, Burns enthusiastically embraced the idea. To his great credit James Johnson quickly realized the real achievement he had made in capturing Burns's collaboration - he was ever anxious to please the poet who, in essence, became the real driving force and editor of the famous *Museum* volumes.

Alas, it was not so with Thomson. He did recognize the genius of Burns, and anxiously enquired of him, in the year 1792, if he would supply lyrics for the grand scheme that he had in mind which was to marry Scottish songs to the finest possible accompaniments, with settings arranged by the greatest composers of the time. He offered to pay Burns for whatever lyrics were sent to him, but this was met with the proud defiance of a patriotic bard:

> As the request you make to me will positively add to my enjoyments in complying with it, I shall enter into your undertaking with all the small portion of abilities I have, strained to their utmost exertion by the impluse of Enthusiasm.....
> As to any remuneration, you may think my Songs either *above*, or *below* price; for they shall absolutely be one or the other.- In the honest enthusiasm with which I embark in your undertaking, to talk of money, wages, fee, hire, &c. would be downright Sodomy of Soul! [7]

The continental composers, such as Haydn, Beethoven, Pleyel, Weber and others, who arranged the music for Thomson, thought a little differently from the poor Scottish Bard, and were well paid for their labours! Burns, for his troubles, received an occasional small gift and the frustration of Thomson's interference in matters of which he wasn't really the equal of Burns in lyric judgement. George Thomson has become the butt of much criticism from editors and biographers of the poet, and much of this has been justified; some, however, has been cruelly exaggerated.

The farmhouse at Ellisland was finally ready to be occupied by May, 1789. The suspicion that the soil would again prove to be his undoing had already begun to haunt Burns. His letters of the period make it clear that, more and more, he was fixed upon the idea of a career in the Excise to secure his future well-being. One of these letters, directed to Excise Commissioner Robert Graham of Fintry, does Burns no credit whatsoever. It was written on 10 Sept., 1788, soliciting for an Excise position at the expense of the incumbent officer. Richard Fowler has put it into the language of simple brutal truth that, Burns was effectively saying to

Graham: "please sack Leonard Smith and let me have his job because I need the money."[8] A proud bard may stand aloof, and dismiss, with disdain, offers of mere cash for his finest lyrics; however, earning a living in the rat race of life could reduce even Robert Burns to the level of unscrupulous mortal! As it so happened, Smith was not discharged to accommodate Burns; a full year elapsed from the period of the letter to Graham, before the poet became an active exciseman on 7 September, 1789.

From the outset at Ellisland Burns was involved in an uphill struggle to derive any potential benefit from the ground. Richard Fowler has delved thoroughly and studiously into the scientific aspects of the soil in all the farms occupied by Burns and his father before him. It puzzled Fowler that Burns seemingly took no notice of advice Riddell and other farmers in the area surely provided:

> Riddell was one of the countryside's notable agricultural improvers, later to receive a silver medal from the Dumfriesshire Agricultural Society in recognition of his achievements. He wrote the *Introduction to the Agricultural Account of Dumfriesshire...* In that *Introduction* he laid emphasis on the benefits to be gained by liming in Nithsdale and Annandale, and one cannot believe that he failed to press this point with Burns the newcomer.[9]

A different angle on Burns's eventual failure to turn Ellisland farm into a viable concern was presented by the writer Alistair Campsie. It was his opinion that Burns was actually set-up at Ellisland; that a conspiracy arose to deprive him of his money from the *Edinburgh Edition,* to weaken his financial resolve, and drive him into dependency on the Excise salary. He would thus be exposed to the watchful eye of a reactionary government determined to crush him at the outset of radical poetry coming from his pen. In truth, Campsie could produce little more than a smattering of circumstantial evidence yet, the Ellisland failure virtually drove Burns into the very bosom of government employment - whether by providence or design, the reactionary forces in Scotland must have been rather satisfied with such an outcome.[10]

At the very time when Burns was thus committing himself to the service of the Excise, he could not resist the temptation to once again offer his satirical pen in the cause of progress, by taking on the bigots of religious intolerance. His good friend William McGill, one of the more enlightened members of the clergy, found himself denounced as a heretic by a group of 'Auld Licht' priests, several of whom had already suffered the poet's scathing derision. The matter had been raised at the General Assembly in May 1789, and McGill was pursued with zealous intent. Essentially a quiet and reserved figure, he was in real danger of being driven from his pulpit and expelled from his profession. To avoid this outcome he was compelled to offer his enemies a humble apology for his enlightened stance, and to desist from further controversy. Burns wrote to his Excise chief, Graham of Fintry, in December, 1789:

> Though I dare say you have none of the Solemn-league-&-covenant fire which shone so conspicuous in Lord George Gordon and the Kilmarnock weavers, yet I think you must have heard of Dr Mcgill.....and his heretical book.- God help him, poor man! though he is one of the worthiest as well as one of the ablest, of the whole priesthood of the Kirk of Scotland, in every sense of that ambiguous term, yet for the blasphemous heresies of squaring Religion by the rules of Common Sense, and attempting to give a decent character to Almighty God and a rational account of his proceedings with the Sons of Men, the poor Doctor and his numerous family are in imminent danger of being thrown out to the mercy of the winter winds. The inclosed Ballad on that business is I confess too local, but I laughed at some conceits in it myself, though I am convinced in my conscience that there are several heavy stanzas in it too.- [11]

The 'inclosed Ballad' was *The Kirk of Scotland's Garland,* and the doctor's clerical enemies such as, Mackinlay and Russell, of Kilmarnock; Moodie of Riccartoun; Grant of Ochilitree; Shepherd of Muirkirk and several others were all roundly hit-off in a rollicking fashion. The ballad opened with:

> ORTHODOX, Orthodox, who believe in John Knox,
>   Let me sound an alarm to your conscience;
> A heretic blast has been blawn i' the West-
>   That what is not Sense must be Nonsense, Orthodox,
>   That what is not Sense must be Nonsense.-

The concluding stanza carried a mock reprimand for the author, being at once replied to with a statement of seeming truth:

> Poet Burns, Poet Burns, wi' your priest-skelping turns,   (drubbing)

> Why desert ye your auld native shire?
> Tho' your Muse is a gipsey, yet were she even tipsey,
> She could ca' us nae waur than we are, Poet Burns, (no worse)
> She could ca' us nae waur than we are.-[12]

The personal religious opinions of Robert Burns have been much debated down through the years. He was surely no more a devout Christian, as some insist, than he was an outright atheist, as proclaimed by other observers of the subject. Richard Fowler has made much of the fact that the poet was deeply impressed by the philosophy of John Locke, and has suggested that an inclination towards deism was the result of Locke's influence on his religious outlook. The anti-clerical satires, the spectacular jibes of *The Holy Fair* being an obvious example (Henley thought the poet, "a hardened and militant anti-cleric"), were written not to attack religion as such, but as a cutting edge to cleave the cant and hypocrisy prevalent within the conservative, 'auld licht' faction, who were entrenched in open, holy warfare against any progressive ideas. On several occasions, however, Burns ventured beyond the bounds of deism into expressions of a more sceptical mode - what today would be described as an agnostic position. A letter written to Mrs Dunlop, on 13 December, 1789, expressed his doubts about the concept of a life after death, regarding such thoughts as perhaps being nothing more than "baseless visions and fabricated fables." Should there be truth in it, however, he would rejoice to be reunited with, among others, his "ever dear MARY, whose bosom was fraught with Truth, Honor, Constancy, & Love."

What was Mrs Dunlop to make of such language? He was barely into the second year of his marriage to Jean Armour; now he can scarcely conceal his "speechless agony of rapture" for his dead love:

> My Mary, dear, departed Shade!
> Where is thy place of heavenly rest?
> Seest thou thy Lover lowly laid?
> Hear'st thou the groans that rend his breast! [13]

In the previous month he had sent Mrs Dunlop a copy of the full song, *Thou Lingering Star,* which he had composed on, or around, the 20 October, the third anniversary of Highland Mary's death. The song was published in Johnson's *Musical Museum - Vol. III,* in 1790, to the air, *Capt. Cook's*

Death, composed by Lucy Johnson, who later married Richard Oswald of Auchencruive. According to James Mackay, the original air for this song was *Mary's Dream;* the practised policy of the *Museum,* however, was not to repeat a tune - *Auld Lang Syne* being an exception - and *Mary's Dream* had already been used for Alexander Lowe's song, *The Moon Had Climb'd the Highest Hill.* Although it eventually became an alternative choice of tune, there is no apparent record of Burns having suggested *Mary's Dream* for this song- Mackay's added claim that the poet used a tune with Mary in its title as a means of concealing the identity of Margaret Campbell, departs from the realms of fantasy, to enter the irrational state of the bizarre! [14]

The struggle to farm Ellisland was finally abandoned by the end of 1791. Burns had given it less than three years before resigning himself to the conclusion that it was "altogether a ruinous business", leaving his future admirers to argue over whether the ultimate failure stemmed from his own lack of ability as a farmer, or on the fact that he had to cut his losses to avoid throwing good money after bad, in a bid to make the grim soil productive:

> This farm has undone my enjoyment of myself. It is a ruinous affair on all hands.- But let it go to hell! I'll fight it out and be off with it.-...
> If once I were clear of this accursed farm, I shall repine more at ease.- [15]

One happy memory of the "accursed farm" was the composition of, what he termed his "standard production in the poetic line" - *Tam o' Shanter.* The claim that the famous narrative was the work of a single day is dubious to say the least. Jean Armour thought that it was, and there is no need to question her integrity. She was not at all literary minded, and the fact that her husband, by the close of the day in question, was able to recite her a poem which he called *Tam o' Shanter,* probably convinced her that the truth of the matter was that he had indeed written it there and then. Yes, but his correspondence makes it clear that he continued to work over the lines, on and off, for some time afterwards, until he was absolutely satisfied that the final version measured up to his demanding level of acceptability for the completed poem. Jean would have been blissfully unaware of the labours it took to complete, and was, therefore, essentially telling the truth when insisting that Rab had set out that particular day on his meander down the Nith, and returned as the author of *Tam o' Shanter.* Does it really matter how long it took him to write it? The end product bears ample testimony to his genius - it is quite magnificent! Within his *ouevre* only *Love and Liberty* comes close to equalling it as a superb literary achievement.

The lease of Ellisland farm was formally renounced on 10 Sept., 1791; in the previous month the crops had been auctioned off amid: "a scene of drunkenness hardly ever seen in this country." Burns himself remained sober - his dogs did not, and they ended up sick and drunk among the riots and squalls that ensued. Fortunately, his wife and family had left for a short break in Ayrshire until it was all over. On the 11 November, Burns moved his family into a town house in Dumfries, a three-roomed apartment in the Wee Vennel, now renamed Bank Street.

The premises next door to the apartment, extending down the lower end of the Vennel along the Whitesands, was a tavern called the Coach and Horses, a house of dubious repute. In the flat above Burns lived George Haugh, the blacksmith (or tinsmith), remembered, in local tradition, for taking Burns's copy of the *Rights of Man* and other radical books, when the poet felt obliged to clear his own house of them until the heat of his political indiscretions blew past. The Distributor of Stamps for Dumfries and Galloway had an office immediately below Burns's house; his name was John Syme. He would, as it turned out, become the poet's closest companion in these remaining years of his life.

CHAPTER TWELVE

The Banks of Nith

There was Maggy by the banks o' Nith, a dame wi' pride enough;
The Five Carlins

I love thee, Nith, thy banks and braes,
Though there Remembrance wakes the tear;
For there he roved that brake my heart,
Yet to that heart, ah, still how dear!
To Thee Loved Nith
by, Maria Riddell

Dumfries has been described as "a compact and rather elegant small town, situated on the Nith, at the point where that river becomes navigable. The environs are generally beautiful; one spot particularly so, where the ruins of Lincluden Abbey Church adorn the peninsula formed by the junction of the *Cluden* with the main river, and this was Burns's favourite musing-haunt." In his political squib, *The Five Carlins,* the poet named Dumfries as "Maggy"- the town being one of five burghs which, at that time, were united in having one member of parliament to represent them:

There was Maggy by the banks o' Nith,   (Dumfries)
   A dame wi' pride enough;
And Marjory o' the mony lochs   (Lochmabben)
   A Carlin auld and teugh: [1]   (tough old woman)

In a later stanza Dumfries is styled as "mim-mou'd (prim-mouthed) Meg o' Nith" - the other three carlins were: Blinkin Bess (Annandale); Brandy Jean (Kirkcudbright), and Black Joan (Sanquhar). The election (1789) was won by the Whig candidate, Patrick Miller, the eldest son of Burns's landlord at Ellisland. The poet, surveying the contest, declared himself "a cool spectator only" - he had no vote to cast, but his sympathies, despite his claim of impartiality, appeared to be in favour of the Tory candidate, Sir James Johnstone:

Up and waur them a', Jamie,   (beat them off)
Up and waur them a';

The Johnstones hae the guidin o't   (have control of it)
Ye turncoat Whigs awa! [2]

The terms Whig and Tory really carried little significance; elections north of the border were, in the main, under the control of Henry Dundas, the right-hand man of Prime Minister Pitt - he it was who made or marred ambitious political figures. Few people had the vote; those who had could barter it off to their own advantage, party allegiance being of little consequence. The result was frequently a foregone conclusion, on deals done with an approving nod from Dundas, who reigned supreme as an uncrowned king.

The poet's career in the Excise was given something of a boost in February 1792, when he obtained a transfer to the Dumfries Port Division. This meant an immediate rise in salary from £50 per annum to £70 - "besides as much rum and brandy as will easily supply an ordinary family" - he had, in addition, perquisites which were worth around an extra £15 per annum to him. Alexander Findlater, his immediate superior in the Excise pointed out, in a lengthy letter to the *Edinburgh Review* in 1834, that Burns was seldom compelled to go beyond the boundaries of Dumfries on Excise business, after his move into the Port Division. One of these exceptions occurred on the 29 February, 1792, when a party of excisemen led by Walter Crawford captured a smuggling brig, *The Rosamond*, at Sarkfoot. Burns had been actively involved, leading a detachment of the group into the actual fray. The real significance behind the incident has, however, centred around the story that Burns subsequently purchased four carronade when the ship's fittings were sold off at an auction in Dumfries, and that he sent them to the French Assembly with his compliments. John G. Lockhart, in 1828, was the biographer responsible for setting this legend in motion; it was challenged by Allan Cunningham in 1834, and controversy has swayed one way or another, ever since. Snyder dismissed it as "a picturesque legend that would do full justice to Gilbert and Sullivan"; however, he was not aware of several important papers which were to surface some two years later. These documents included Walter Crawford's journal, John Lewars's inventory of the auctioned items, and Burns's account of the cost in preparation for the auction. In the *Burns Chronicle* (1934), the famous historian, Henry W. Meikle's article, *Burns and the Capture of the Rosamond,* swayed several scholars to accept as fact that Burns had attempted to dispatch the guns to France. Of the poet's recent major biographers, James Mackay is almost convinced about the truth of the incident, Ian McIntyre appears to remain a shade more sceptical.[3]

The real truth of the carrondade incident would certainly have been known to Alexander Findlater, the Excise Supervisor in Dumfries at the time it allegedly took place. If there had been no truth in it, then Burns's boss was surely the person ideally qualified to squash the persistent rumours. In his letter to the *Edinburgh Magazine*, Findlater, broaching on the subject concerning, "Burns purchasing, and sending to the French Directory, four guns, captured in a smuggling vessel", refused to be drawn into elaborating on the precise details, making his position on the matter quite clear, by declaring that there could be no further comments, "into a technical, and, of course, disagreeable discussion of Excise forms of business, not at all likely to be interesting to the public".[4] The lack of an emphatic denial says much!

The carronade incident may not have been directly responsible for the enquiry which the Excise Board set up to investigate the poet's politics, but it hardly helped his situation. James Mackay states that: "There was certainly no question of his actions being called to account by his Excise superiors." It is quite true that a passage of time, some eight months to be precise, elapsed between the incident and the actual investigation into whether or not Burns was a person "disaffected to Government". It is difficult, however, to accept that eyebrows were not raised over the guns business, in official places, and a watchful presence thereafter assigned to the democratic poet. He had enemies in and around Dumfries, and he knew it; a certain, "envious, malicious devil" had made mischief by "raising a little demur on (his) political principles". He had been suspected of proposing disloyal toasts; had been reported as a member of the audience during a political disturbance in Dumfries theatre; and, towards the end of the year, he and his friend Robert Riddell subscribed to a newly founded radical newspaper the *Edinburgh Gazetteer.*

As an employee of His Majesty's government unquestioned loyalty was expected of him - there were now people in authority who reasoned that they had their man - this poet of the people was now about to fall from the security of his Excise perch. Burns, however, had no intention of sacrificing the well being of his young family on the rock of reactionary gossip. He had friends in high places and decided to make use of them. None was more valued than Robert Graham of Fintry. He wrote two well-constructed, if somewhat emotionally-charged letters, to Graham seeking his assistance in the matter; care was taken to remind the Excise Commissioner that they were both Royal Arch masons. Graham, no doubt, suspected the truth of the matter; he would have seen through the pleading of loyalty, where the loyalty was, to say the least questionable, but he decided that a friend in need, with a young family to support, was worth protecting. Burns was not even officially censured, though he was severely reprimanded and warned as to his future conduct. The outcome of it all brought forth one of the best letters he ever wrote. John Erskine of Mar, having been wrongly informed that Burns had been dismissed, made enquiries on his behalf with a view to setting-up some form of assistance for him.

John Erskine's grandfather, the sixth earl and eleventh Lord of Mar, had led the Jacobite rebellion of 1715. Recorded in history as Bobbing John, because of the frequency in which he had changed sides prior to finally committing himself to the Stuart cause, Mar had suffered the loss of his estates and title by Act of Attainder on the rebellion being crushed. His grandson, eventually had the title restored as the seventh earl. John De Lancey Ferguson wrongly named him as the twenty-seventh earl, and many writers, including Mackay and McIntyre have followed suit - some attention should have been paid to Robert Chambers, an authority on Jacobitism, who gave Mar his correct title. One splendid passage in Burns's letter to Erskine of Mar, despite its frequency of previous quotation, deserves further billing:

> Does any man tell me, that my feeble efforts can be of no service; & that it does not belong to my humble station to meddle with the concerns of a People? - I tell him, that it is on such individuals as I, that for the hand of support & the eye of intelligence, a Nation has to rest. - The uninformed mob may swell a Nation's bulk; & the titled, tinsel Courtly throng may be its feathered ornament, but the number of those who are elevated enough in life, to reason & reflect; yet low enough to keep clear of the venal contagion of a Court; these are a Nation's strength.- [5]

Burns requested John Erskine to commit this letter to the flames; he had the fear of it being read by someone who, on getting, "the least knowledge of the picture.....would ruin the poor Bard for ever." Although Findlater objected to Allan Cunningham stating that the Excise Board had treated Burns harshly; that it was "highly coloured" to suggest that they had ordered him "not to think", and, "to be silent and obedient" - 'Honest' Allan was hardly to blame: Burns himself had informed Erskine that William Corbet, Supervisor-General of Excise, had used these very words in the reprimand that was handed out to him at the conclusion of their enquiry.

The political views of Burns have been discussed, at length, in the major biographies, and also in separate articles and essays. He has been portrayed as a Tory, Jacobite, Jacobin, Nationalist, and even as a Socialist - though chronologically the latter is impossible! Few writers have matched Dr W J Murray of La Trobe University Melbourne for his penetrating insight into the poet's politics, published in 1979. From the outbreak of revolution in France, in 1789, down to the two letters imploring Graham's intervention, Dr Murray has astutely observed Burns's situation:

> Yet in all the surviving poems and correspondence there is no mention of the French Revolution before 1792. It is likely that some of the manuscripts relating to this period were lost or destroyed, but this does not explain why *none* of them found their way into print, especially when those of the much more dangerous period after 1792 did. Nor does Burns's severe illness explain anything, for it did not prevent his writing innocuous pieces relating to domestic politics. What probably did affect his attitude, however, was his appointment to the Excise at the beginning of September of that year. The job entailed up to 200 miles a week on horseback, a physically demanding task; but more significantly it made him a government man in the most unpopular of posts. Nevertheless it was a position Burns actively sought, and he owed it to friends in high places: indeed this was the politics that was eating away at Burns's creative genius: the politics of Patronage and Place.....
> His appointment to the Excise through the favour of people in power was more than a taste of the bitter pill of patronage, however, for it placed a bridle on the democratic tongue of one who was now a King's man.[6]

The frustration of a bridled tongue was the price being paid by Burns in order to provide some substance for his wife and little ones. The most explosive event in his lifetime - the fall of the Bastille heralding a democratic revolution in France, had passed with ne'er a whisper from an apostle of liberty! The "glorious privilege of being independent" stretched well beyond the means of people like Burns who were being cramped by an oppressive regime. Any study of his politics, whilst taking due consideration of what he actually said, also requires an educated guess at what he yearned to shout aloud!

At the beginning of the year of his political troubles Burns first met Maria Riddell, a young lady, then in her late teens, who was to figure fairly prominently in the latter days of his life. She was married to Robert Riddell's brother Walter; her own name being Woodley, her husband had bought the estate of Goldilea near Dumfries, which he at once renamed Woodley Park in her honour. Burns was much impressed with her beauty and charms: that she was "a votary of the Muses", capable, claimed Burns, of writing poetry "much beyond the common run of the Lady Poetesses of the Day", naturally delighted him. He gave Maria a letter of introduction to the printer William Smellie, in the hope that the diaries she had kept during a period spent in the West Indies - where she had met Riddell - might be published . Maria's father had been the Governor and Captain-General of St. Kitts and the Leeward Islands.

By the following month Burns was acknowledging a letter from Maria as "the welcomest letter I ever received" - his reply, opening with the bold address, "My Dearest Friend", treated her to the news of his £20 per annum salary increase, with: "Perquisites.....worth 15 or £20 more. So rejoice with them that do Rejoice." [7] He was soon a frequent visitor to Woodley Park; the large library which Riddell owned was an attraction, but it doubtless came a poor second to Walter's foremost jewel, the gorgeous Maria!

> Maria, all my thought and dream,
> Inspires my vocal shell:
> The more I praise my lovely Theme,
> The more the truth I tell.-[8]

In the autumn of the year 1792 Burns's thoughts again returned to his past love of Mary Campbell. Three years previously, on the third anniversary of her death, he had written *Thou Lingering Star* - he now composed its companion piece, a song which proved to be the only occasion in which he would ever refer to her as Highland Mary. The two songs were immensely popular throughout the Victorian era of the 19th century, and obviously did much to generate the cult of Mariolatry which pervaded Burnsian circles during that time. He sent his song to George Thomson who replied with enthusiasm:

> Your verses upon 'Highland Mary' are just come to hand: they breathe the genuine spirit of poetry and, like the music, will last for ever. Such verses, united to such an air.....might form a treat worthy of Apollo himself. I have heard the sad story of your Mary: you always seem inspired when you write of her.

How on earth Thomson could suggest that Mary Campbell always seemed to inspire Burns is a complete mystery. Of five songs concerning her, the best of them, *Afton Water,* treated her almost casually whilst singing the praises of the stream and its locality. Thomson had, in fact, rejected one of the others, *Will Ye Go to the Indies,* as being substandard. There were, apparently, several other songs written for her by Burns, but none of them have survived.[9]

By the end of the 19th century the cult which had aspired around her fame began to crumble. Henley, in his brilliant, though controversial essay, scorned Robert Chambers for having done much to install Highland Mary as, "the heroine-in-chief", within the legend of Burns:

> .....that heroine-in-chief is a girl of whom scarce anything definite is known, while what may be reasonably suspected of her, though natural and feminine enough, is so displeasing to some fanatics, that, for Burns's sake (not hers) they would like to mythologise her out of being; or, at the least, to make her as arrant an impossibility as the tame, proper, figmentary Burns, the coinage of their own tame, proper brains, which they have done their best to substitute for the lewd, amazing, peasant of genius, the inspired faun, whose voice has gone ringing through the courts of Time these hundred years and more, and is far louder and far clearer now than when it first broke on the ear of man.[10]

Henley was ever adept at bruising people's toes though he had but one foot to stamp with. His amputated limb and supporting crutch had, of course, served his friend Stevenson with the idea of Long John Silver for his classic story of pirates and treasure. When Henley accused RLS's wife of plagiarism, and ignored the novelist's demands for an apology, it was, as they say, the end of a beautiful friendship. There is no doubt, however, that Henley had a grasp of Burns, man and poet, excelled by few, and some compliments to his fellow minstrel were extremely flattering - praising Burns as having "well nigh the finest brain conceivable" and regarding him as "the most exquisite artist in folk-song the world has seen". This did not, however, free Henley from the barrage of criticism directed at him from the bardolaters, one of whom laid aside the contentious essay and thanked his God that, at least it had not been written by a Scotsman!"

Henley's scoffing remarks about the bronze statue of the Coilsfield dairymaid being erected at Dunoon, were as nothing, compared to the rumours which began to circulate regarding her personal character. She had first of all, been totally confused with an unmarried mother of the same name, who lived in Dundonald parish. Even as this error was being completely nailed, talk was heard of a testimony, which had been long suppressed, given out by Burns's one time friend John Richmond. This had accused Mary of cavorting with James Montgomerie during the very period of her attachment to Burns. Richmond claimed that he and others had warned Burns that she was deluding him, but he refused to accept their warning, and only after they gave him "ocular proof" of her sharing a room with Montgomerie did Burns take heed. It was then hoped that he would shun her, but alas, claimed Richmond, the poet returned "like a dog to its vomit". No evidence supports Richmond's absurd tale, and it should be pointed out that he was a notorious liar. James Montgomerie, the alleged lover of Mary Campbell, was the sixth son of Lord Eglinton; he was four years older than Burns, who regarded him as both friend and masonic brother.

As it so happened, Montgomerie was involved in a local scandal of sorts, at this time and place, with a woman named Campbell. When she bore him a love-child, her irate husband sued him at law, and Burns, who seemed sympathetic to Montgomerie's plight, caught the heated exchange of the lawyers in his fragment, *Extempore in the Court of Session.* Whether

Richmond's memory, in the lapse of years, had utterly confused the Montgomerie-Campbell scandal, or whether he was indulging in malicious fabrication against Highland Mary, will never now be known - those who are prepared to give credence to his gossiping drivel can live with their irresponsible fantasies. As for Montgomerie, after the court case he left Scotland to pursue a military career in the West Indies, where he eventually became Governor of Dominica. Burns, in the early draft of his poem, *Passion's Cry,* fondly imagined it as expressing Mrs Campbell's manner of writing to the father of her love-child.

The period of Burns's later life, the 1790's, was almost exclusively devoted to songwriting. There were exceptions, such as *The Rights of Woman; The Address Spoken by Miss Fontenelle; The Ode for Washington's Birthday* and sundry fragments. Of his political songs written during these years *Scots Wha Hae* (1793), and, *A Man's A Man for a' That* (1794-5), have proved their worth by their enduring popularity. The song, *A Man's A Man,* first appeared in *The Glasgow Magazine* for August 1795. According to J R Tutin, as stated in his series of Newbery Classics, a copy of the song had been inscribed in a 1794 *Edinburgh Edition,* which appeared, verbatim, in *The Oracle* for 2 June, 1795.[12]

The humorous songs of Burns have also proved to be immensely popular - *The Deils Awa wi' th' Exciseman; Duncan Gray; Last May a Braw Wooer* and such - it is, however, his exquisite love-songs for which he is most highly regarded in his art; *Bonny Wee Thing* in praise of Deborah Duff Davies; *Wilt Thou be my Dearie,* being among many written for Jean Lorimer; *O, Wert Thou in the Cauld Blast* for Jessie Lewars, the young woman who nursed him in his final illness. Some songs, wrongly attributed to him, have, over the years been removed from the canon. Some have remained as his, though he really only polished them up from collected pieces. Conversely, attempts have been made to deprive him of the lyric gem, *Ca' the Ewes,* by harking to an Ayrshire tradition claiming one Isabel Pagan as its author.[13] Burns took the idea of the song from the Revd. John Clunie, the minister of Ewes, Dumfriesshire; he added verses of his own and mended the middle two, not for the better, in the opinion of some scholars. If Pagan had any part in the song, why was it not included in her works, published in 1805? Such an omission is evidence against her authorship; further proof being that her doggerel verse renders it unlikely that she was capable of producing such a song as *Ca' the Ewes.*

The two songs which best express Burns's genius are, *A Red Red Rose,* and *Auld Lang Syne;* both appeared in the *Musical Museum, Vol. V.* 1796, the year of the poet's death. They, had, however, been composed much earlier - *Auld Lang Syne* as far back as 1788. In both cases controversy exists as regards their originality, and of how much Burns drew upon extant verses. Several phrases used in *A Red, Red Rose,* were certainly taken from previous works; Henley goes as far as to state that "every single stanza - exquisite examples of his art though all four be - is borrowed." The song should, therefore, have been signed 'Z' in the *Museum* signifying it to be the reworking of previous material; it was signed 'R' which indicated Burns's own compostion. The mistake lay with James Johnson. The songs from which Burns drew his inspiration were, however, rather poor effusions; can it really be said, despite the clear resemblence, that the following lines can match Burns?

> Her cheeks are like the Roses
> That blossom fresh in June,
> O, she's like a new-strung instrument
> That's newly put in tune.

Few impartial judges would deny Burns his authorship of the song, when comparing the above trash to the immortal lines:

> O MY LUVE's like a red, red rose,
> That's newly sprung in June;
> O my Luve's like the melodie
> That's sweetly play'd in tune.-

A similar pattern emerges with *Auld Lang Syne,* and it was signed 'Z' in the *Museum.* The origins of the song can be found in James Watson's *Comic and Serious Scots Poems* (1711):

> Should old Aquaintance be forgot,
> And never thought upon,
> The Flames of Love extinguished,
> And freely past and gone?

The full song consists of ten, eight-line stanzas. A later version appeared in Allan Ramsay's *Tea-Table Miscellany* (1723), and two ballads expressing opposition to the Union of Parliaments in 1707, also carry the sentiments of "old long sine". Examining these works against the version of *Auld Lang Syne* as we now recognize it, the eminent Burns scholar, G. Ross Roy, came to the conclusion that:

> Obviously Burns can have found in these songs but a phrase here and there; most of what we have is surely his own:

> > For auld lang syne, my jo,
> > For auld lang syne,
> > We'll tak a cup o' kindness yet
> > For auld lang syne.

> "Burns knew instinctively that he had created a masterpiece and he has been proven right. At every New Year's Eve much of the world sings Burns's greatest song, even those who have never heard his name or who cannot read the immortal words they sing, with a mixture of hope for their own futures and that of a world united in brotherhood." [14]

CHAPTER THIRTEEN

Heresies In Church And State

The shrinking Bard adown the alley skulks,
And dreads a meeting worse than Woolwich hulks,
Though there, his heresies in Church and State
Might well award him Muir and Palmer's fate.

From Esopus to Maria.

On the 21 January, 1793, the French Jacobins executed King Louis XVI; just over one week later, on 1 February, the Convention declared war on Great Britain. The English revolutionary, Thomas Paine, had made an impassioned direct appeal within the body of the Convention, for the King's life: "Kill the monarchy, but spare the man" was the gist of his plea; not only was it contemptuously spurned, but Paine himself now fell under the suspicion of the hardline Sansculottes, a faction led by the fanatical Marat. At the end of 1792 Paine had been tried, *in absentia*, in London, on a charge of seditious libel - not treason, as some writers have declared - and outlawed from England for ever. He had already settled in Paris where he had been elected to the Convention as the member for Calais.

Another voice raised in a last desperate attempt to prevent the King being guillotined was that of Thomas Muir, a young Scottish advocate from Huntershill near Glasgow - an enthusiastic follower of Paine, who had found himself in trouble with the authorities for distributing and propagating Paine's book - *Rights of Man.* It is known that Burns obtained a copy of the book, and quite obviously, became much influenced by it. He also possessed a copy of the equally famous book - *Common Sense.* This had been written by Thomas Paine, and published in January 1776, during his period in America - it had provided the people there with so much political inspiration - the spark which ignited an outright demand for full independence!

On the 18 February, 1793, William Creech published a second *Edinburgh Edition* of Burns's works. Among those who were favoured with a gifted presentation copy was Nancy McLehose - Clarinda! She had sailed from Scotland to the West Indies, after her affair with Burns had ended, in an attempt to reconcile herself with her estranged husband. Her stay there lasted less than three months. Viewing his lifestyle with his dusky mistresses, convinced her that it was futile to place any further faith in saving her troubled marriage. Burns was delighted at her return to Edinburgh and wrote:

> Shall I hear from you? - But first, hear me! - No cold language - no prudential documents - I despise Advice, & scorn Controul - If you are not to write such language, such sentiments, as you know I shall wish, shall delight to receive; I conjure you, By wounded Pride! By ruined Peace! by frantic disappointed Passion! By all the many ills that constitute that sum of human woes - A BROKEN HEART! - To me be silent for ever !!! - If you insult me with the unfeeling apothegms of cold-blooded Caution, May all the - but hold - a Fiend could not breathe a malevolent wish on the head of *My* Angel! - [1]

He attempted to dismiss the language of this epistle as: "the fustian rant of enthusiastic youth." At the age of thirty-four, he was surely stretching the point of credibility.

During the early period of 1793 the poet was completely immersed, in his limited free time, on work for George Thomson's *Select Collection,* and the first set of this was published on the first of May. The renowned Burns editor, James Kinsley, described the collaboration between Burns and Thomson as, "this uneasy alliance between a true artist in folk-song and a stiff-necked refiner" - the phrase related much truth! Twenty-five songs appeared in this first part of Thomson's ambitous scheme, six of these being the work of Burns, including, *Open The Door to Me, Oh.* This song contained the lines W.B. Yeats regarded with much admiration, even if he did misquote them in his appreciation:

> The wan moon sets behind the white wave,
> And time is setting with me, Oh:

James Mackay seems to think that Kinsley omitted the song from his three-volume edition of Burns, this is not so: it is given by that editor as No.403. Thomson published it with the comment, "Altered by Robert Burns"; however, Henley & Henderson stated in their songnotes, that no old ballad had ever come to light which resembled, *Open The Door to Me, Oh!*, leaving no reason at all to doubt it as wholly an original Burns song.

A political poem entitled, *On The Year 1793*, has recently come to light as the result of researches made by a modern Burns scholar, Patrick Scott Hogg. He discovered it in the pages of the *Edinburgh Gazetteer* of 8 January of that particular year. It was subscribed with the pseudonym *Aratus* - a Greek astronomical poet, and a word having a common root and resemblance to aratoris, the Latin for ploughman. Inevitably, it raised the question, had these verses been written by Robert Burns, the ploughman poet?[2] The poem has no great literary merits, though this fact alone does not prohibit the prospect of Burns as its author. The date of its publication must also weaken the case. At this very period Burns was under the intense pressure of the Excise Board's enquiry into his political conduct. One of several incidents prompting this action was their knowledge that he had supplied the radical *Gazetteer* with two of his poems. Henley & Henderson, and James Mackay, in their respective editions, have stated that he also had the song, *Here's A Health to Them That's Awa*, published in that newspaper, but of this there is no conclusive proof. At any rate, Burns, now aware of the Excise Board's intentions, would surely have been acting in a rash, even foolhardy manner, to have dispatched another political piece to the 'paper, whilst under the full glare of the Board's surveillance. Saving his Excise career was Burns's pressing priortity at this precise time, and furnishing Johnston's *Gazetteer* with further political tracts, was hardly a step in that direction. The newly discovered poems will occupy Burns scholars with interest and debate for sometime to come; however, *On The Year 1793*, cannot pass as one of the better examples.

One of the known *Gazetteer* pieces, *The Rights of Woman*, was sent, by Burns, to Mrs Elizabeth Graham of Fintry, on 5 January, 1793. A copy was sent to her husband, the Excise Commissioner, on the same day. The poet took great pains to point out that it had nothing to do with politics, and the "rights" he advocated: *Protection, Decorum,* and *Admiration* certainly bear testimony to his statement. The attempts to place Burns in the forefront of the feminist cause, on the strength of these lines, are, therefore, rather exaggerated, though the poem did open, and close, with a bold political impact.

By July of 1793, Thomas Muir, who had broken the conditions of his bail by journeying to Paris, decided to return home. Born on 24 August 1765, Muir had been educated at Glasgow Grammar School and followed on to the university in the same city; completing his studies at Edinburgh, he was then admitted into the Faculty of Advocates on 24 November, 1787. As an elder of the Church of Scotland, he had fought a long and protracted battle against the conservative elements within it, finally resigning his eldership, and immersing himself in radical politics as a disciple of Paine. A passport description of Muir describes him as, 5ft. 9ins. tall, red hair, blue eyes, high forehead, with round chin and long face. James Smith, a Glasgow arms dealer, who became friendly with Muir in Paris, wrote to the Glasgow branch of the Friends of the People movement:

> I had the honour to dine with Mr. Maxwell and Mr. Muir - We met him by mere accident in a coffee house in the Palais Royal. We had all the fashionable dishes, with variety of wines.....All perfectly quiet here since the death of the king.....much safer than Glasgow, no robberies, or pickpockets.....women very well dressed.[3]

Smith indicated that they had just been to visit Helen Maria Williams (a correspondent of Burns's), and had also visited Thomas Christie of Montrose, whose *Letters on the French Revolution,* was one of many 'replies' to Edmund Burke's *Reflections* - the most famous being, Paine's *Rights of Man,* and, James Mackintosh's *Vindiciae Gallicae.* The Mr Maxwell, referred to in Smith's letter, was Dr Willam Maxwell, who had been a member of the National Guard responsible for escorting King Louis to the scaffold on that fateful January day. Maxwell, in the following year, settled in Dumfries, where exciseman and poet, Robert Burns, was soon describing him as his, "most intimate friend".

Thomas Muir, on his return journey to Scotland, called en route at Ireland, to make known his position to the revolutionary group, the United Irishmen. He had intended to make for Edinburgh, but it was inevitable that, on landing at Portpatrick after sailing across from Dublin, it would only be a question of time before he was arrested. The Sheriff of Stranraer reported: "Muir was apprehended here on his way from Ireland. He seems a good deal confused re the idea of Stranraer Jail till he is conveyed to Edinburgh." On Sunday 4 August 1793 he was taken from the jail, clapped in handcuffs and leg-irons, and taken by coach to the capital city to await his trial. The date, 4 August, makes a complete nonsense of the ludicrous story that Burns was in Gatehouse when Muir passed through. Some versions stretch to the extent that Burns actually saw the captured reformer bound in his restraints. The fact is that Burns and his friend Syme had already returned from their sojourn in the Border country: they had arrived back in Dumfries on Friday, 2 August.

Henry Erskine was approached by friends of Muir to defend him at his trial; he willingly agreed, but Muir refused the offer, being anxious to conduct his own case, in his own manner. It made little odds one way or another to the verdict, nothing other than guilty was possible - the trial a mere pretence of justice. The sentence, however, sent shock waves through the reform movement - fourteen years penal servitude in Botany Bay. A clear lesson was being served upon anyone who dared to challenge the tyranny of Henry Dundas, Scotland's uncrowned king! In the following month the Revd. T F Palmer was tried on the charge of writing an address against the war with France - he was sentenced to seven years transportation. The historian, W H Meikle, put it thus:

> These trials evoked widespread indignation. Jeffrey and Sir Samuel Romilly, who were present in court, were horrified at the conduct of the judges. In France, the account of the proceedings deepened that hatred of England to which Kersaint had given expression in the National Convention in January, when he eulogised the zealous Scottish defenders of the principles of the French Revolution "who were meriting the honour of being persecuted by the British Government."[4]

Down in the Scottish border town of Dumfries Robert Burns had followed the events with dismay - sheer frustration must have pervaded his democratic soul, and still the fear that, if he dared loose that 'bridled tongue' he would, quite conceivably, "be awarded Muir and Palmer's fate". Yet, he had to do something - and thus he produced, and forwarded to George Thomson the lyrics of *Scots Wha Hae*, indicating in his covering letter that his expressed sentiments equally applied to contemporary events:

> By Oppression's woes and pains!
> By your sons in servile chains!
> We will drain our dearest veins,
>   But they *shall* be free!

Lay the proud Usurpers low!
Tyrants fall in every foe!
LIBERTY'S in every blow!
Let us DO OR DIE!!![5]

George Thomson was wildly enthusiastic by way of reply: "Your Heroic ode is to me the noblest Composition of the Scottish language." Burns had composed the verses in August 1793. On the 16 September, a poem appeared in the *Edinburgh Gazetteer,* titled: *The Ghost of Bruce.* The spirit of the 14th century warrior king, making himself known to the poet, laments the enslaving of Scotland by the English government, but advises him to let the people know that, "Your Country in her breast stills carries Bruce, / And ne'er shall be enslav'd." The poem, written in blank verse, does not appear at all to be in the mould of Burns, the self-styled RHYMER Rab. He had composed a few, mostly unsuccessful pieces, in this format, and the claim that the lines were the work of Burns, was met with some scepticism. The case made by Partick Scott Hogg (whose researches unearthed the poem) in favour of Burns's authorship is a compelling one, and the impartial enquirer would be wrong to reject it, pending a full study of Scott Hogg's entreaty to have Burns recognized as the author.[6]

In all, over twenty poems have been put forward by Scott Hogg as the possible work of Burns, submitted to, and published anonymously, by various newspapers of the period when Burns had been effectively silenced. They are certainly the most intriguing find in Scottish literature since the discovery of the Mavisgrove manuscripts by James D Law, in 1903. Law discovered these papers at Mavis Grove, which had been the residence of Colonel Arent De Peyster (1736-1822), the Commanding Officer of the Dumfries Volunteers which Burns joined in January 1795. He was addressed, by Burns, in the poem opening with: "My honour'd Colonel, deep I feel"; and later, at the poet's funeral, he led the Volunteers in the final tribute to their colleague.

Although the Mavisgrove papers have been dismissed by such notable editors as Kinsley and Mackay, as nothing more than yet another attempt to foist off inferior verses as the work of Burns, the opinion of Robert D Thornton tells a different story. Prof. Thornton, a recognized authority on the songs of Burns, has stated that several of the Mavisgrove songs: *Elibanks and Elibraes; Ever to be Near Ye;* and, *To Mr Gow Visiting*

Dumfries, among them, may well be genuine works of Burns. "Who shall decide when doctors disagree?" The most controversial piece discovered by Law was the poem given only in James Barke's edition of Burns - *Look Up and See* - which Law printed privately regarding its profanity as being too daring to risk general publication:

> The best piece is unfortunately in too profane a vein for general circulation. It is a satire of twenty-one Sempiltonian stanzas, purporting to be a reply to David Sillar, who had rebuked Burns for his frequent flippant rhyming references to King David the Psalmist, and shows R. B. on his Biblical and bardic mettle with crushing effect. Each verse to Sillar terminates with the refrain *"Look up and See,"* which is also the title of the daring Epistle. From its references to Goudie, and from other allusions, the period of compostion must have been about 1786.[7]

Although Law maintained that: "Several expert Burns students to whom this satire has been submitted concur with me in saying it is unquestionably a characteristic product of the Ayrshire poet's racy pen", there is little basic doubt that Burns had nothing whatsoever to do with its compostition. In the aftermath of Law releasing it in private copies, the text was printed in an obscure freethought magazine. The poem, like other controversial works such as *The Tree of Liberty,* has retained a measure of prominent popularity it does not really deserve.

The war which the French republicans had declared on Britain raged on throughout 1793. Indeed, with the exception of Russia, and a few neutral states, France was virtually at war with the rest of Europe. In the early summer the course of the revolution within France had intensified when a Sansculottes' inspired struggle succeeded in driving the moderate faction, the Girondins, from their tenure in the Convention, and thus delivered control of the French Republican armies into the hands of Robespierre's Jacobins. Dumouriez quit his post as a leading Republican general deserting to the ranks of the Royalists - and Burns sarcastially commented:

> You're welcome to Despots, Dumourier;
> You're welcome to Despots, Dumourier.-
> How does Dampiere do?
> Aye, and Bournonville too?
> Why did they not come along with you, Dumourier? [8]

The Marquis de Dampierre, second-in-command to Dumouriez, and Beurnonville, Minister of War, refused to follow the general as he (and the allied forces) had hoped, and both remained within the ranks of the republicans.

The enemies of Burns, then as now, tended to regard him as being far too pro-France in his political stance, thus, in effect, opening himself to charges of disloyalty towards his own government. There is no doubt that he disliked the Tory administration of William Pitt; even more so, he had nothing but sheer contempt for the reigning royals, the House of Hanover, but his loyalty to his country and people were never at all in serious doubt. As with Charles J Fox, and the radical Whig party that he led, the poet's position was one of complete opposition to the war itself. His comment to Mrs Dunlop: "War I deprecate, ruin and misery to thousands are in the blast that announces the destructive demon", and several of his poems and songs such as: *Logan Braes; Nature's Law; When Wild War's Deadly Blast; I Murder Hate by Field or Flood,* make it quite clear that Burns was an anti-militarist; the poet who yearned for the brotherhood of man, as Burns did, would have been nothing less than sickened by the very thought of conflict and slaughter on the battle-field. - Whilst others thanked God for a great national victory, Burns chose to differ:

> Ye hypocrites! are these your pranks?
> To murder men and give God thanks?
> Desist for shame! Proceed no further:
> God won't accept your thanks for Murther.[9]   (Murder)

As the end of 1793 approached, the authorities in Scotland made a further attack upon the democratic societies. Two prominent London delegates, Joseph Gerrald and Maurice Margarot, attending a Convention in Edinburgh, were arrested on 5 December, along with William Skirving, secretary of the Edinburgh societies. All three at their subsequent trials received the same sentence as Thomas Muir. Richard Fowler pointed out in his (1988) book on Burns, that two members of the jury at Gerrald's trial were well known to the poet - William Creech, his publisher; and the bookseller Peter Hill. Gerrald, whom one historian declared as "the most eloquent person ever to appear in a Scottish dock", strongly objected to Creech being on the jury - needless to say, the trial judges, with the notorious Lord Braxfield as Lord Justice Clerk, swept Gerrald's valid objection aside, with arrogance and contempt.

At the same time as the seditious trials were taking place in Scotland, the proprietors of the *Morning Chronicle* were facing similar prosecution from the courts in London. They, however, were given an acquittal, the jury refusing to convict them on the charge of printing a seditious address. In the following March, Burns allowed this newspaper to publish *Scots Wha Hae* - on condition that they did not reveal him as the author - when the editor , James Perry, asked the poet to join the newspaper staff, at a wage reputed to be five guineas per week, Burns felt that he had to decline the offer in the interests of his family's security.[10] Burns promised, however, to furnish the newspaper with, "any bagatelle that I may write", if an address, "safe from these spies with which he may be certain that his correspondence is beset", could be made available. It was this phrase that sent Patrick Hogg to search the columns of the *Chronicle* and other newspapers of the time, to see if Burns had been as good as his word. Hogg is in no doubt that Burns did so, and has backed his claim by producing his book as the crucial evidence.[11]

It has long been fashionable to name Alexander Wilson, the weaver poet, as the author of any anonymous radical material, by those who seem anxious to protect Burns from involvement. It should be noted, however, that Wilson had a contempt for the authorities almost in the spirit of his hero, Thomas Paine, and he was, therefore, more than likely to scorn the very idea of lurking behind a cloak of anonymity. After serving a term of imprisonment for writing seditious verses, he left Scotland in disgust at what he saw as the very throttling of liberty, to start a new life in America. He eventually found considerable fame, and presidential recognition, not as a poet, but as an ornithologist.

A letter from Burns to John McMurdo, Chamberlain to the Duke of Queensbury, contained the first hint relating to the famous collection of bawdy songs which became known as *The Merry Muses*. This letter was dated in John De Lancey Ferguson's two-volume edition of 'The Letters', as December 1793, and therein lies an interesting feature of how the poet's first editor, James Currie, could tinker misleadingly with the text. De Lancey Ferguson added that, the text was copied straight from Currie, the MS had not been traced. Burns informed McMurdo:

> I think I once mentioned something of a collection of Scots
> songs I have for some years been making: I send you a perusal
> of what I have got together. I could not conveniently spare them
> above five or six days, and five or six glances of them will
> probably more than suffice you. A very few of them are my own.
> When you are tired of them, please leave them with Mr. Clint of
> the King's Arms. There is not another copy of the collection in
> the world; and I should be sorry that any unfortunate negligence
> should deprive me of what has cost me a good deal of pains.....[12]

The manuscript, however, was subsequently traced; the letter had
actually been "tentatively dated Februray 1792", and Currie had taken it
upon himself to make some textual alterations, and had deliberately added
the thoroughly misleading sentence: "A very few of them are my own."
Ross Roy, in bringing this liberty of Currie's to light, admitted that for years
he had been baffled by the editorial meddling - why had Currie, assuming
he was attempting to prevent common knowledge of Burns's vulgarity - not
just destroyed the offending letter? He had, after all, made sure that other
offensive pieces did not grace the pages of his edition. The answer provided
by Ross Roy more or less completes the story; Currie became aware that
the collection had appeared in book form shortly after Burns's death - the
only course was, therefore, to insert the sentence "A very few of them are
my own" as a well-meaning, yet pathetic attempt, to whitewash Burns's
reputation.[13]

At the very close of the year 1793 an incident took place which was
to cause Robert Burns a considerable amount of personal anguish. Much
has been written about the fracas which arose at the home of Robert Riddell
during an evening of much merry-making which climaxed with some of the
men proposing, as a means of livening the proceedings, an acting-out of
the *Rape of the Sabine Women.* Catherine Carswell, in her biography of
Burns, has explained the event in a manner which may not be too far
removed from the truth:

> At New Year a hideous thing happened, which to this day is
> attributed in Dumfries to a 'rag' on the part of gentlemen
> wearing the King's uniform and bent upon amusement at the
> expense of a too haughty poet whose 'hands were not
> altogether clean of the coom of Jacobinical democracy.'

The drinking of the evening had left Burns fired-up to a degree of reckless abandonment: Carswell continued:

> To each stalwart Roman a Sabine was allotted. The only poet among them should take his hostess. A man was a man for a' that! Robert was already primed. It would not be the first kissing frolic in which he had taken the lead.....when Robert had carried out his part in the hearty despatch and all the latitude the occasion called for, he was stupefied to find himself alone.....The whole thing was a trick, and what it now came to was a question of class. A gauger in liquor had affronted Mrs. Riddell of Glenriddel. *This* was unprecedented and unforgivable.....
>
> Class, after all, is class. Robert left the house disgraced.[14]

A well-composed written apology proved useless - the Riddells, and their friends in Nithsdale wanted no further truck with Robert Burns. Carswell possibly had the wrong woman - it seems more likely that Burns's *Sabine* would have been Maria Riddell, whose husband Walter was not present - the other facts are, however, of more importance. Had army officers, "epauletted puppies", as Burns styled them, taken advantage of a drunken poet to bring him down a peg or two? Had Maria, who doubtless frolicked with him away from prying eyes, been utterly mortified at the audacity of a common gauger making amorous advances towards her in full view of her fellow-gentry? The answer to both questions must ring of the positive. Maria's husband being absent, his brother, Robert Riddell, took his part and made it clear to Burns that he was to leave the house and never return; his behaviour towards a lady apparently condemned as outrageous!

The fact that Burns, when subjected to being cold-shouldered by the Riddells and other members of the Dumfries gentry, retaliated by directing some ill-tempered epigrams at Maria and Walter, would seem to indicate that Maria, and not Elizabeth Riddell, had been the woman involved with him in the drunken set-up at Riddell's home. Robert and Elizabeth Riddell were never subjected to the poet's subsequent wrath over the matter. There is little doubt however, that his apology was sent to Elizabeth - a gesture in keeping with the fact that she was the hostess of the ill-fated evening.

The physical hangover suffered by Burns was the least of his troubles, the mental one was much more sustaining: the drunken incident at Friars' Carse at once deprived Burns of the stimulating intellect of Robert Riddell, and also the delights of his flirtatious friendship with Riddell's sister-in-law, the flaunting Maria. The New Year of 1794 had approached spring when some shocking news came to him that his friendship with Riddell could now never be repaired - the laird of Glenriddel had died! The date of his death was 24 April; by June his family home, Friars' Carse, scene of fond memories for Robert Burns, was on the market for sale.

By now Burns was turning the full attention of his Muse on a young woman he had known for several years, but who now suddenly seemed to turn his head as only the select few had done; he became totally, and completely, infatuated with her. In due course she inspired more love-songs from his pen than any other woman had done; her name was Jean Lorimer - after a few false starts at adorning her with an Arcadian title, he finally settled on the designation of Chloris. Her flaxen ringlets - lintwhite locks in the vernacular - now brightened the gloom of many a dismal day in Dumfries.

CHAPTER FOURTEEN

The Lintwhite Locks of Chloris

LASSIE wi' the lintwhite locks,
Bonie Lassie, artless lassie,
Wilt thou wi' me tent the flocks,
An wilt thou be my Dearie O.-

Lassie Wi' the Lintwhite Locks

Chloris, at worst, you'll in the end
But change your lover for a friend

Sir George Etheredge (1635-91)

In his biography of Jean Lorimer: *Burns's "Chloris" A Reminiscence*, Dr James Adams, M.D., has listed no fewer than thirty-one poems and songs, by Burns, which he claimed the poet had written on behalf of this remarkable woman. It is far in excess of the material for any other of his heroines, and more than double the number in which Jean Armour is honoured. The first of these was the song, *Craigieburn-wood*, initially composed in the year 1791, but revised during the winter of 1794, and in fact Jean's birthplace was Craigieburn, close to Moffat. Burns had actually drafted out the original verses in response to a plea from John Gillespie, a fellow-exciseman, one of several young men who had fallen under the spell of Jean's striking appearance, crowned by the glory of her luxuriant pale yellow (flaxen) hair.

Her father, William Lorimer, had leased a farm from Robert Riddell at Kemmishall, not too far removed from Burns's farm at Ellisland, and the pair had struck up a sound friendship. After his move into Dumfries Burns continued to call at the Lorimer home when out and about on his Excise rounds. The aspersions cast on the farmer as a smuggler were fully dispelled by James Mackay in his biography of Burns - previous writers had confused the issue by coming-up with the wrong William Lorimer.

The summertime of the year found Burns in full swing with his work for George Thomson's *Select Scottish Airs* - this despite Thomson's chosen composer, Ignaz Pleyel, appearing to be caught up as an innocent hostage of the events in Paris, which prompted Burns to write the editor of the songs a rollicking letter:

> Is there no news yet, my dear Sir, of Pleyel? - Or is your work to be at a dead stop, untill these glorious Crusaders, the Allies, set our modern Orpheus at liberty from the savage thraldom of Democratic Discords? - Alas the day! And woe is me! That auspicious period, pregnant with the happiness of Millions - that golden age, spotless with Monarchical innocence & Despotic purity - That Millenium, of which the earliest dawn will enlighten even Republican turbulence, & shew the swinish multitude that they are but beasts, & like beasts, must be led by the nose & goaded in the backside - these days of sweet chords & concords seem by no means near![1]

The letter was accompanied by a copy of the splendid verses opening: *When Princes and Prelates and het-headed zealots,* which could not then be published - the political and sexual language deeming them offensive - they are now included in most modern editions of Burns.

The poet had made it perfectly plain to Thomson that he needed the inspiration of "admiring a fine woman; & in proportion to the adorability of her charms, in proportion you are delighted with my verses." He was, however, anxious that the music publisher should be aware that the latest goddess of his Muse was merely by way of "the guileless simplicity of Platonic love." To his Excise superior, Alexander Findlater, he made mention of Chloris, a name he appears to have taken from Sir Charles Smedley's *Child and Maiden* (1668):

> Ah, Chloris! that I now could sit
> As unconcerned as when
> Your infant beauty could beget
> No pleasure, nor no pain!

The name thus settled, in preference to the alternatives that he had flirted over, such as, Sylvia; Celia; Cloe and Lesbia, the songs began to flow. The best of them, however, made no mention of her name either as Chloris or as Jean. Indeed, the song, *Lassie Wi' the Lintwhite Locks* made mention only of Cynthia, in the fourth stanza, a symbolic reference to the moon, it being the surname of Diana, Roman goddess of light; the name taken from Mount Cynthus, where, as told in the deeds of mythology, she had been born:

> As Cynthia lights, wi' silver ray,
> The weary shearer's hameward way,
> Through yellow waving fields we'll stray,
> And talk o' love, my Dearie O.[2]

Had Burns recalled his usage of the songbook *The Lark* (1765), where the line "Bright Cynthia silvered all the plain" occurs in Vol.I, p.89? Of the air, *Rothiemurchie's Rant,* to which the lyrics of *Lassie Wi' the Lintwhite Locks* was set, Burns declared that it "put him into raptures." Thomson didn't appear to be quite so enthusiastic about it!

The spell of Chloris dominated Burns's love-songs throughout the remainder of 1794, and well into the following year. Rather surprisingly for an editor of the poet's *Complete Works,* James Mackay has stated that, Burns wrote no further songs for Chloris after January 1795, the last being, *Sweet Fa's the Eve on Craigieburn,* and made very few references concerning her after that date. He noted that Burns had, however, on 2 August 1795, written to George Thomson:

> Did I mention to you, that I wish to alter the first line of the English song to Leiger m'choss, alias The Quaker's wife, from, "Thine am I, my faithful Fair," - to "Thine am I, my Chloris fair?" If you neglect the alteration, I call on all the NINE, conjunctly & severally, to anathematise you! [3]

Mackay thereupon criticizes Thomson for annotating this letter to the effect that Burns, from this period, disapproved of the name Chloris altogether. The facts centring around all this appear to be at variance with Mackay's opinions. There were songs written in praise of Chloris after January 1795 including: *Why, Why Tell Thy Lover; Yon Rosy Brier; Long Long the Night; Forlorn My Love; Mark Yonder Pomp of Costly Fashion; Their Groves o' Sweet Myrtle; 'Twas Na Her Bonie Blue E'e; O, This is no' My Ain Lassie,* and, of course, the amended version of, *Thine Am I.* The annotation made by George Thomson in his copy of the letter from the poet seems justified, since Burns himself informed the music publisher, in February 1796:

> In my bypast songs, I dislike one thing; the name, Chloris. I

meant it as the fictitious name of a certain lady; but, on second thoughts, it is a high incongruity to have a Greek appellation to a Scotch Pastoral ballad....What you once mentioned of "flaxen locks" is just: they cannot enter into an *elegant* description of beauty.[4]

Thomson had commented that he could "scarcely conceive a woman to be a beauty, on reading that she had lintwhite (flaxen) locks." Yet, Burns himself thought that: "Golden locks are a sign of amorousness" and, Dr Adams, who met Chloris prior to writing about her, gave her hair colour as pale yellowish lemon - abundant and of glossy sheen. The name, as the poet stated, came from Greek mythology; Chloris was a daughter of Amphion and Niobe.[5] Pausanias claimed that Chloris (Pale) was merely the name given to Meliboea when she turned pale from fright. Appollo and Artemis slaughtered Niobe's children - some sources say all ten, alternative legends claim that Chloris, and one brother survived. She married Neleus the king of Messiana, who was so enraptured by her alleged beauty, that he had journeyed to Boeotian Orchomenus to wed her. According to Pausanias, Chloris was one of the winners of the Heraean games.

The Chloris of Burns's songs however, lived no enchanting legend, but had rather a bleak and unpleasant life. Whilst still in her teens she foolishly eloped with a worthless rake named Whelpdale, in March 1793; a few months later Whelpdale being pursued for heavy debts abandoned her, and fled to his native Cumberland. He eventually ended up in prison as a debtor, and Chloris saw nothing further of him for twenty-three years, and then an attempted reconciliation fell flat. According to the Chambers-Wallace edition of Burns:

It has been said that this poor, unprotected woman was at length led into an error which lost her the respect of her friends. She is stated to have spent some time in a kind of vagrant life, verging on mendicancy, and never rising above the condition of a domestic servant. About the year 1825, a gentleman, to whom she had made her poverty known, bestirred himself on her behalf, and told her sad case in the newspapers in the hope of raising a subscription for her relief.[6]

The gentleman's wife sent Chloris some of these newspapers and received, from her, a letter of due acknowledgement. Shortly afterwards

Chloris managed to find employment as a housekeeper in Newington, and in this situation it is somewhat gratifying to note that she was at least treated in her last years with a measure of comfort by a beneficent employer. She contacted an illness suspected of being tuberculosis, and at Middleton's Entry, Potterrow, she died in September 1831 in her fifty-seventh year. A memorial was erected over her grave in the Preston Street cemetry in 1901, a gesture by the Ninety Burns Club.

The revised version of *Craigieburn-wood,* sent by Burns to Thomson in January 1795, certainly was not the last song for Chloris; more than likely, *O, That's the Lassie o' My Heart,* has this honour. A copy of this was enclosed in a melancholy letter, January 1796, sent to his Edinburgh friend Robert Cleghorn. Burns indicated that the song had been composed a little earlier. In his celebrated edition of *The Songs of Robert Burns,* James C. Dick, has tentatively dated it as autumn 1795. This letter to Cleghorn reiterated the sad news regarding the death of his little daughter, Elizabeth Riddell, born in the year 1792, during the full flush of his friendship with the occupants of Friars' Carse:

> Since I saw you, I have been much the child of disaster. - Scarcely began to recover the loss of an only daughter & darling child, I became my self the victim of a rheumatic fever, which brought me to the borders of the grave. - After many weeks of a sick-bed, I am just beginning to crawl about.[7]

The reference to an "only daughter" presumably meant by his wife; he had, of course, two illegitimate daughters, both of whom, strangely enough, were also named Elizabeth - "dear-bought Bess" was still in the care of his family at Mossgiel; whilst Anne Park's daughter had been taken into his own household at Ellisland, and Dumfries. The birth of a son on 12 August, 1794, had provided Burns with the opportunity of paying compliment to his patron, - "the man to whom I owe all that I am and have!" - the Earl of Glencairn, who had died three years previously - the boy being named James Glencairn Burns.

Towards the end of the year 1794 Burns found himself promoted in the Excise to the role of Acting Supervisor for Dumfries. At around the same period the first steps appear to have been taken to repair the broken friendship with Maria Riddell. He addressed her, in the third person, by a letter on a "Friday Eve", which De Lancey Ferguson ascribes to January 1795.

> Mr. Burns's compliments to Mrs. Riddell - is much obliged to her for her polite attention in sending him the book. Owing to Mr. B- being at present acting as Supervisor of Excise, a department that occupies his every hour of the day, he has not that time to spare which is necessary for any belle-lettre pursuit; but, as he will in a week or two again return to his wonted leisure, he will then pay that attention to Mrs. R-'s beautiful song "To thee, lov'd Nith," which it so well deserves.[8]

He added a P.S. "Mr. Burns will be much obliged to Mrs. Riddell if she will favor him with a perusal of any of her poetical pieces which he may not have seen."

Sometime during the latter period of 1794 Burns began the composition of the song which has endeared him to political radicals throughout the world - *A Man's A Man For a' That,* and his biographer, James Mackay, has captured the full essence of its sentiments by commenting, in a language slightly leaning on Yeats: ".....this song ranks among the top ten of Burns's lyrics; technically flawless, brilliant in phrasing and burning with passionate intensity, it has assured the poet's international reputation beyond anything else he ever wrote." The story related by Mackay, concerning the fate of Karl Liebknecht, the German Communist Leader, facing a firing squad in 1919, with the words of the song on his lips, is pure fantasy - Liebknect was not executed by firing squad. A rumour did circulate to the effect that he had been shot in 1915, four years prior to his actual death, but it proved false - biographies ought to reflect known facts, and sufficient biographical material exists on Liebknecht to relate the story correctly, thus avoiding idle speculation - *"Facts* are cheels that winna ding, / An' downa be disputed:"

There is little doubt that, *A Man's A Man for a' That,* was the prose sentiments of Thomas Paine's *Rights of Man* expressed in rhyme. The parallels between these works have been given in several sources, Thomas Crawford's excellent *Study of the Poems and Songs - Appendix II,* being well worth consulting. The comments made by Henley and Henderson regarding this outstanding song did them but little credit; their sarcasm and

Tory prejudice could hardly be suppressed:

> LIke *Scots Wha Hae* - ('the Scottish *Marseillaise':* Whatever that may mean) - this famous song - ('the *Marsellaise* of humanity': whatever ***that*** may mean) - .....is very plainly an effect of the writer's sympathies with the spirit and the fact of the French Revolution, and of that estrangement from wealthier loyalist friends, with which his expression of these sympathies and his friendship with such 'sons of sedition' as Maxwell had been visited.[9]

The opening days of 1795 were, in fact, to prove of some consequence to the poet. A letter to William Stewart of Thornhill requested the loan of three guineas, as the "accursed times, by stopping up Importation (had) lopt off a full third part of (his) income" which, as he said, with his large family to support, left him in a distressing manner. Another letter, to Capt. John Hamilton, also spoke of this bleak situation, confirming that his "otherwise scanty income" had now been reduced by no less than £20. He enclosed to Hamilton the three guineas borrowed from Stewart, as a part of a debt he promised to settle soon in full. On 12 January he completed a letter first started on 20 December, 1994, which estranged his friendship with Mrs Dunlop.

Doctor John Moore, to whom he had addressed his autobiographical letter in 1787, had expressed his regret at the executions of the French King and Queen. Burns, quite rightly, had taken Moore to be a political liberal whose acquaintance, and regular dining dates with Thomas Paine and Lord Lauderdale, during his stay in Paris, had identified him with the spirit of reform. In an apparently tactless manner Burns now ventured forth to Mrs Dunlop, who had members of her family married to French royalist emigres recently fled from the bloodlust of the revolutionaries, that: "the honest Doctor's whining over the deserved fate of a certain pair of Personages", simply could not meet with his approval:

> What is there in the delivering over a perjured Blockhead & an unprincipled Prostitute to the hands of the hangman, that it should arrest for a moment, attention, in an eventful hour, when, as my friend Roscoe in Liverpool gloriously expresses it-
>
> "When the welfare of Millions is hung in the scale
> And the balance yet trembles with fate!"

> But our friend (Moore) is already indebted to People in power, &
> still looks forward for his Family, so I can apologise for him; for
> at bottom I am sure he is a staunch friend to liberty.- Thank God,
> these London trials have given us a little more breath, & I
> imagine that the time is not far distant when a man may freely
> blame Billy Pitt, without being called an enemy to his Country.[10]

The letter was given only in part by Dr Currie, in his Edition. It was published in full by De Lancey Ferguson, from a MS in the Esty collection held at Ardmore, Pennsylvania. Ferguson has commented that: "the year is written in, not in Burns's hand, as 1795, which is impossible." The fact that the letter carried over from December 1794, with parts added both on the 1st and 12th of January 1795, probably led to the error. The trials referred to by Burns were those of Thomas Hardy and J Horne Tooke for High Treason, in October, 1794, and also that of John Thelwell in December. All were acquitted; the packed-jury system which had delivered the radicals into the clutches of the government in Scotland, did not operate south of the Border with similar effect. At Horne Tooke's trial, Prime Minister William Pitt had, in fact, suffered the humiliation of being subpoenaed as a witness for the defence.

On the 31 January Burns enrolled as a founder member of the Dumfries Volunteers - an action which his radical admirers have seemingly felt obliged to explain, under pressure from those elements of conservative Burnsians, who have viewed his move as their consolation that the poet, after a burst of revolutionary fervour, had, in his final years, turned to the loyal roll-call of King and Country when it really mattered. W J Murray, in his admirable study of the poet's politics, has pointed out that the concern for the welfare of his young family led Burns down this path; the invasion scare had put radicals into an invidious position, their loyalty tested in the full glare of the political spotlight - none more so than those who depended on the government for employment:

> I hae a wife and twa wee laddies,
> They maun hae brose and brats o' duddies;   (food and clothes)
> Ye ken yoursels my heart right proud is,
>   I need na vaunt;   (boast)
> But I'll sned boosoms and thraw saugh-woodies (tackle menial
>   Before they want.-   tasks)

These were the pressing concerns that reduced Burns, at the beginning of 1795, not to menial labour, but to joining the Dumfries Volunteers. Burns took out further insurance against political persecution by writing a song for the Volunteers that appeared in the *Courant* and other papers in May of that year. Of all the songs and poems Burns wrote, 'The Dumfries Volunteers' is that which conservatives seize on when they want to claim him for their cause. This song is not anti-revolutionary, however, but anti-French.[11]

Burns's action and his patriotic song must, therefore, be analysed against the course of events in France. The day of the Sansculotte and the war cry of *Ça ira* was fading fast; the men of property moved with brutal speed to protect their ambitious plans. The mob had carried through the revolutionary purpose of ridding them of a reactionary monarchy and a redundant aristocracy; the French bourgeoisie, as Cromwell had done in Britain in the previous century, were anxious to discipline the mob into taking the course of revolution no further along the democratic path. This counter-revolution to the Jacobin ideals resulted in the executions of Robespierre, Saint-Just, and Couthon at the end of July 1794; within a few days, a further eighty-seven Jacobins perished by the guillotine, and the people were left without effective leadership. The way was now open for the strong man to take the helm; by 1799, Napoleon Bonaparte's remarkable rise to power finally killed the dream of liberty, equality, and fraternity. The "haughty Gaul" who threatened Britain in 1795, was not the Jacobin Republic of France, but a transitional Directory, pending Napoleon's dictatorship. Dr Murray, has put the matter into its proper perspective by comparing the verses for the Dumfries Volunteers, *Does Haughty Gaul Invasion Threat,* with another song of the same period:

At the same time as Burns was throwing out this sop to the establishment, he was writing the song that has been seen as the International of World Brotherhood; 'For a' that, and a' that'. It is a song that includes many of the thoughts of the young Burns, shorn of their resignation and acquiescence: rebellious and defiant, it pictures a goal to be achieved.[12]

This, plus the letter which estranged his long friendship with Mrs Dunlop, should satisfy the most demanding enquiry into the real nature of Burns's politics during this penultimate year of his life. His head could direct him to suppress the republican sentiments which might jeopardize his family's welfare, but the rebel streak which he could never quite contain, occasionally surfaced, despite the fact that nobody knew better than he did, just how dangerous such expressions were, especially from one whose every utterance would have been carefully scrutinized. His dexterity in walking that precarious political tightrope, and putting his message across, whilst holding the threatening reactionary elements at bay, was, to say the least of it, quite remarkable.

CHAPTER FIFTEEN

Bold John Barleycorn

Inspiring bold **John Barleycorn!**
What dangers thou canst make us scorn!

Tam o' Shanter

I love drinking now and then. It defecates the standing pool of
thought. A man perpetually in the paroxysms and fevers of
inebriety is like a half-drowned, stupid wretch condemned to
labour unceasingly in water, but a now-and-then tribute to
Bacchus is like the cold bath - bracing and invigorating. -

Robert Burns.

Very few persons whose fame has subjected them to the scrutiny of
biographical detail, have had their drinking habits so thoroughly examined
as Robert Burns. The conclusions are equally remarkable having ranged
from one extreme to another. He has been claimed as "a veritable model of
sobriety", - and has also been written off as having been "burnt to a cinder".
His last years in Dumfries are allegedly the period when his craving for
alcohol had increased to the extent that, according to some sources, it was
a factor in ruining his health, and bringing his life to a premature close.

The drinking had started early enough in life; by his own admission,
during the summer spent at Kirkoswald in 1775 - or was it 1777? An
unknown hand had altered his own earlier given date, in the text of his
autobiography, to push it forward in time by a year or two - an attempt to
convey that John Barleycorn had not chanced upon him at such a tender
age? - Who knows! By the time he had his MSS ready for his *Kilmarnock
Edition* in 1786, he had composed his ode in lavish praise of whisky:

> O thou, my MUSE! guid, auld SCOTCH DRINK!
> Whether thro' wimplin worms thou jink,   (flow thro' spiral coils)
> Or, richly brown, ream owre the brink,   (froth over)
>   In glorious faem,
> Inspire me, till I *lisp* an' *wink*,
>   To sing thy name![1]

The companion piece to *Scotch Drink - The Author's Earnest Cry and*

Lament, had also been composed in good time to grace the pages of the *Kilmarnock:*

> SCOTLAND, my auld, respected Mither!
> Tho' whyles ye moistify your leather, (occasionally)
> Till when ye speak, ye aiblins blether; (maybe talk nonsense)
>   Yet deil-mak-matter!
> FREEDOM and WHISKY gang thegither,
>   Tak aff your whitter.[2] (take a hearty dram)

The *Cry and Lament* had been inspired by what was seen as an unjust tax imposed on Scottish distillers. On the same issue Burns had addressed an open letter, to Prime Minister William Pitt, which was published in the *Edinburgh Evening Courant* on the 9 February, 1789, and signed with the pseudonym, *John Barleycorn - Preses.* The general tendency has been to regard these pieces as nothing more serious than a bout of play-acting on Burns's part - a mere dash of patriotic wit. Surely only the more extreme wing of teetotalism would venture to rebuke the poet for glorifying his love of drink, on the strength of these verses. As James Mackay has noted, "there is no evidence of Burns as a drinker, far less a 'bout alcoholic' in (the period) 1784-5." This, in reply to Alan Bold's claim: "Burns's remark that 'occasional hard drinking is the devil of me' is a classic confession of bout alcoholism."[3]

There is no doubt that Burns, in common with most young men, frequented the pubs around his home district with his friends of that particular time. The Whitefoord Arms in Mauchline appears to have been a favourite haunt of the young poet, and doubtless he spent many a happy evening there in the company of Richmond, Smith and Hunter. A social drink, however, is not hard drinking in the accepted sense, and in any case, despite its relative cheapness of these times, the lack of money was ever a compelling problem with Burns, and only a limited amount would have been available for the tavern.

By the time he had moved to Edinburgh, however, he became involved with a totally different set of players in vastly different surroundings. Membership of the Crochallan Fencibles brought him into the company and companionship of men who were, by any given standards, worshippers of Bacchus. The advocate Charles Hay, who later became the judge, Lord Newton could boast that, "Drinking is my profession the law merely my amusement." Burns's own group within the Fencibles included the three Williams - Nicol, Dunbar and Smellie, and it takes little stretch of the imagination to accept that a convivial evening in their company, would leave in its wake, many a well-drained glass, and empty bottle.

In the aftermath of Edinburgh, in his early days in Nithsdale, Burns was a frequent visitor at the fireside of Robert Riddell who valued his reputation as a tippler sufficiently to enter into the drinking contest celebrated in Burns's excellent production *The Whistle* - the poet, in the role of mere spectator, declared:

> A bard was selected to witness the fray,
> And tell future ages the feats of the day;
> A bard who detested all sadness and spleen,
> And wished that Parnassus a vineyard had been.[4]

It would beggar belief to consider that Burns and Riddell would not spice their conversations at Friars' Carse over many a dram, and according to tradition, Burns liked to be fortified with a large one for the road, on a dark wintry evening, when the time came to make his way back along the murky tracks to his farm. On the occasions when he stayed overnight at the home of Patrick Miller, the poet apparently stipulated for a bottle of brandy in his bedroom, "and drank it well nigh out before the morning." His biographer, James Mackay, disputes the truth of this story on the grounds that there is no evidence of Burns spending the night at Miller's house, the relationship between the pair being not at all cordial. The story, if it was based on idle gossip, would render Mackay's counter-claim valid; however, names can be named! The information was passed to Sir Walter Scott by Miller's son, the MP whom Burns entrusted with placing *Scots Wha Hae* anonymously in a London newspaper.[5] The truth cannot now be known, though the question should be raised as to whether it can be justified to condemn Patrick Miller jnr. as a wilful liar, in order that Robert Burns be spared another facet of his drinking habits? As regards the relationship between Burns and Miller senior, it was friendly enough with the exception of a limited period during the poet's disenchantment with Ellisland farm.

There have been several instances reliably given of drinking causing Burns considerable embarrassment. The evening at Friars' Carse from which the resultant quarrel with the Riddells emerged; an incident at the home of his friend McMurdo in which his old enemy, the Devil, as Burns himself described it: "taking advantage of me being in drink.....tempted me to be a little turbulent." The incredible escapade, first raised by Robert Thornton, when John Lewars and Burns, trying to walk off the effects of a night's hard drinking, became caught up in a fracas with two local servant girls, which landed Lewars in court facing charges of "crimes of a heinous nature." [6] The letter from Robert Ainslie to Clarinda admitting that he and Burns had ended up roaring drunk; the political clash with Capt. Dods in January 1794 when Burns's toast, with the reference to the conflict with France, "May our success in the present war be equal to the justice of its cause" was deemed by the enraged army officer as "obnoxious" - and the pair of them almost fell upon the business of murdering each other, was explained away as "a drunken squabble."

In his edition of Burns's letters John De Lancey Ferguson has declared that, "for every apologetic or defiant reference in the letters to drunkenness, there are a dozen or a score to ill-health." Whatever Ferguson's reasoning, the fundamental truth of his statement was challenged by Richard Fowler, who came up with a reference list of drinking in no fewer than thirty-six letters, concluding in a ratio closer to, one to two, than one of twelve or twenty. Fowler also made out a case that Burns may have exposed himself to lead poisoning through his habit of drinking cheaper wines, thus possibly absorbing lead from the litharge added to the wines to kill the vinegar fly. [7]

This prompted a counter-claim from James Mackay that no trace of lead was found in the hair sample of the poet which had been subjected to medical analysis in 1971. This was hardly surprising, since no test for lead was carried out! The process of neutron activation analysis, carried out by doctors Lenihan and Smith, at Glasgow University, was specifically to test for mercury - a separate examination would have been required to determine the presence of lead. Mackay, in the role of devoted bardolater, nevertheless took a real heavy swipe at Burns's Australian biographer:

> It should be noted, however, that Fowler subscribed to the view that Burns was a habitual wine drinker who, on many occasions, drank to excess; so it seems we are back to the old *canard* of drunkenness. Doubtless this perverse view will continue to be

Canard is not a particularly pleasant word, the more so when emphasized by italics. If Robert Burns was fond of drinking then that was very much his affair; it was essentially a part of his lifestyle, and it ought to be told in his biographies; there is little to be gained by attempts at diverting the truth, and hurling accusations of a "perverse view" at those who stand by the rather convincing evidence. The viewpoint that his drinking was exaggerated because it did not interfere with his duties as an exciseman, and his songwriting for George Thomson and James Johnson, has but limited credibility. As Catherine Carswell noted, Prime Minister Pitt, and his henchman Henry Dundas, drank far more than Robert Burns, and they, for heaven's sake, were running the country. Argued that they were making none too successful a job of it is probably justified, but their excessive drinking was not at all the root cause of the nation's woes.

Ironically, James Mackay, who seems so anxious to protect Burns from the reputation of a tippler, 'involved' him in a drinking session which never took place. Sir Samuel Egerton Brydges wrote a fantasy autobiography in which featured a purely imaginary visit to the poet at Ellisland farm. Brydges's imagination had Jean Armour dutifully producing a bottle of whisky and two glasses, from which he and Burns drank numerous toasts. Brydges was, in fact, writing of an ideal visit in the format of *Laudor's Imaginary Conversations* with ancient Greeks and Romans; Mackay, and James Kinsley, however, took him at face value, and assumed that a visit had actually taken place. Even more absurdly, Mackay stated that Brydges visited the poet in the company of John Ramsay of Ochtertyre. Needless to say, Ramsay makes no mention whatever of Brydges; indeed he makes it clear that his only companion in his Ellisland visit, was the Revd. Stewart of Luss.[9]

Whatever else may be said of Burns and the subject of drink, there can be no denying that one of his convivial evenings with cronies Willie Nicol and Allan Masterton, produced one of the finest drinking songs ever penned. Burns related its background thus:

> The air is Masterton's, the song mine. The occasion of it was
> this:- Mr. William Nicol, of the High School, Edinburgh, during the
> autumn vacation being at Moffat, honest Allan - who was at that

time on a visit to Dalswinton - and I went to pay Nicol a visit. We
had such a joyous meeting, that Mr Masterton and I agreed....
that we should celebrate the business.

> O WILLIE brew'd a peck o' maut,   (large quantity of ale)
>> And Rob and Allan cam to see;
> Three blyther hearts, that lee lang night   (whole evening)
>> Ye wad na found in Christendie   (Christendom)

Scott Douglas primly pointed out that, as the song reaches its glorious
final stanza, the penultimate line carried "a gross blunder", when printed in
Johnson's *Musical Museum*, which had the further misfortune to be
transcribed to subsequent editions - the stanza in question reads:

> Wha first shall rise to gang awa,
>> A cuckold, coward loun is he!   (cowardly fellow)
> Wha first beside his chair shall fa',   (fall)
>> He is the king amang us three! [10]

This gives rise to the notion, wrote Scott Douglas, that Burns's idea
of a joyous evening was: "a struggle to get dead-drunk before the rest, and
thus be crowned 'king of the company!'". He amended the line to read,
"Wha *last* beside his chair shall fa'", and the whole impact of the poet's
humour was totally lost. Henley & Henderson thankfully put the matter to
rights by pointing out:

> Writing to Captain Riddell, 10th October 1789, on the Whistle
> day, Burns quotes two stanzas, and in quoting Line 3 changes
> 'first' to '*last'*; but that he italicises the word shows that he
> made the change to suit the special circumstances of the
> contest. 'First,' too, is found in Johnson, in the earlier Editions
> of Currie, and in a quotation of the stanza in a letter to
> Alexander Cunningham. There is, therefore, no warrant for the
> supposition that it is either (a) misprint or clerical error. [11]

Doctor Currie, it can be added, moralized that, the three blythe hearts
who had sampled Willie's peck o' maut: "all men of uncommon talents, are
now all *Under the turf.*" Dr Currie has been branded "the arch calumniator"
for having landed Burns with the reputation of a tippler. In fact Currie, who
met Burns but once, very briefly in a Dumfries street, was preceded by
Robert Heron, who knew the poet slightly better, and who weighed in with

an essay on his life, prior to the Currie biography. Heron, like Currie has been subjected to much abuse by admirers of Burns; however, it is often overlooked by their detractors, that both men also lavished much praise on the poet. Others have duly accepted the praise whilst rejecting the criticism. With regard to the essay by Robert Heron, an interesting opinion on this attitude has been raised by Ian McIntyre:

> It is still widely held that (Heron) deliberately set out to blacken Burns's character and that he, along with Dr Currie, was responsible for the belief that the poet was driven to an early grave by drink.....
> The well-known passage.....about how the Kilmarnock edition was received, for instance, is frequently cited with approval, and so is the perceptive tribute in which Heron asserts that Burns exercised a greater power over the minds of men by his writing 'than has been exercised by any half-dozen of the most eminent statesmen of the present age'. If that is thought to be well observed, it is not clear, on a dispassionate view, why Heron's account of the deterioration in Burns's behaviour should be dismissed out of hand.[12]

The testimonies supplied by James Gray and Alexander Findlater for a biography of Burns published in 1815 are frequently quoted as proof that his drinking has, to say the least of it, been greatly exaggerated. Gray was a senior teacher at Dumfries Academy during the period 1794-1801; he is principally recorded in the story of Burns as the tutor of his son Robbie, and also as a fellow member of the Dumfries Volunteers. Beyond that he appears to have had little social intimacy with the poet. He later married Clarinda's friend Mary Peacock, and became Principal of Belfast Academy in 1822. Gray's glowing character reference of the "Exciseman-Saint" which Henley found it "impossible....to believe in" might well have brought a blush of embarrassment to the Bard's own countenance had it been produced during his lifetime.

Alexander Findlater would certainly have been well aware of Burns's social habits, and his testimony is, altogether, a much more balanced account than Gray's panegyrical tract. It did exonerate Burns to an extent, and made it clear that he never reported for his Excise work whilst under the influence of drink. Findlater nevertheless conceded that: "when he (Burns) sat down in an evening with a few friends whom he liked, he was apt to prolong the social hour beyond the bounds that prudence would dictate." He also conveniently chose to overlook that his friendship with Burns was, in the poet's own words, "well watered with many a bottle of good wine." The most questionable aspect of their respective testimonies was the unaccountable delay. Why the lapse of fifteen years after Currie's initial charges of excessive drinking, before Gray and Findlater decided to put pen to paper in defence of Burns's character?

The noticeable deterioration in the general health of the poet by the spring of 1795 - his very appearance seems to have reflected a change for the worst - certainly cannot be attributed to alcohol as the sole cause. His role as Acting Supervisor in the Excise, in Findlater's absence, burdened him with an excessive workload during a period of extremely inclement winter weather; the labours of songwriting for Johnson and Thomson took considerable toll, whilst the pressing anxieties about the future security of his young family haunted him as concerns for his health increased. Small wonder that the solace of the bottle proved too tempting on the demanding occasion:

> Gie him stong Drink until he wink,
> That's sinking in despair;
> An' liquor guid, to fire his bluid,
>   That's prest wi' grief an' care:
> There let him bowse an' deep carouse,
>   Wi' bumpers flowing o'er,
> Till he forgets his loves or debts,
>   An' minds his griefs no more.[13]

Despite all these pressures he simply couldn't resist involving himself in the by-election for the Stewartry of Kirkcudbright. He decided to support Patrick Heron, and wrote two ballads in his favour, adding a third to celebrate his triumph at gaining the seat. Heron has been accepted, by editors and biographers of Burns, without question, as the Whig candidate who took on the Tory establishment of Lord Galloway and his allies, and left them languishing in ignominious defeat. This story has continued down from the time of the election itself, and no doubt was inspired by Burns's own contribution, in citing Heron as "the independent commoner" and "the honest man" whilst pouring scorn on the opposition camp.

The truth is that Patrick Heron was no Whig - he was a Dundas man to the core, a fact verified from the Sidmouth MSS in which Dundas made it clear to Henry Addington (Lord Sidmouth), that Heron was surpassed by none "as a respectable gentleman and friend of government in the House of Commons." Dundas had, in fact, entered into a pact with Heron regarding the election of 1795, as a means of returning his gratitude, "for Heron's services in combating the Scottish reform movement of 1792". In the end, Heron was returned unopposed, though some Burns editors seemed to be under the illusion that Thomas Gordon of Balmaghie, his opponent, had insisted on forcing the by-election to a ballot.

Why then did Burns support Heron, and write such a glowing account on his behalf? The only answer can lie in the fact that he was seeking political backing to advance his Excise career, and knew that none would be forthcoming from the opposition camp headed by the Earl of Galloway. He detested the earl, as the epigrams on him make clear, though no reason has ever surfaced to explain the bad blood between them. It is known from a letter written by Burns to Heron that he tentatively solicited the politician's influence; thus, when all was said and done, Burns and Heron had found a mutual pact, and one which allowed the poet the undoubted pleasure of firing off political squibs, on Herons's behalf, at people in the Galloway camp, for whom he had neither time nor respect.

Heron again stood in the general election of the following year, and again Burns's pen was made available. On this occasion the opposition did push the contest to an actual vote, and again Heron won the day. His career came to an end in 1803, when his opponent in the election held in the previous year, Montgomerie Stewart, accused him of a breach of rules, namely, that he had omitted the names of entitled freeholders, erased others, and received illegal votes in the election for praeses, in favour of Richard Oswald and against John Gordon of Kenmure. Heron attempted to square the issue by conceding four votes to Stewart, and discounting his own personal one; this tied the candidates at 41 votes apiece, the clincher falling to Gordon of Kenmure, whom Heron had attempted to remove from the voting role. Needless to say, Gordon, with his vote restored, cast it against Heron who was then unseated. It has been presumed that Dundas was a bitterly disappointed man, from the comments made in a letter he wrote to Addington, regarding the mess of the Stewartry of Kirkcudbright contest.[14]

As for Heron himself, he died on his way home from London, in the wake of these battles, 9 June, 1803, aged sixty-seven. He had hardly merited the lines form Burns's pen:

> For a' that, and a' that,
> Here's Heron yet for a' that;
> A House o' Commons such as he,
> They wad be blest that saw that.[15]

The mid-summer of 1795 brought news of the death of William Smellie, the printer, and the friend who had introduced him to the Crochallan Fencibles; by August his friendship with Maria Riddell was more or less fully restored, and he can be found teasing her in a manner akin to charming satire, chiding her for the sway that she holds over her enslaved male admirers:

> *You* a Republican! - You have an Empire over us; & you know it too: but the Lord's holy name be praised, you have something of the same propensity to get giddy (intoxicated is not a lady's word) with power; & a devilish deal of aptitude to the same blind, undistinguishing FAVORITISM which makes other Despots less dangerous to the welfare & repose of mankind than they otherwise might be.[16]

Whatever may be made of his own republicanism, he appeared to be conscientious enough in his membership of the Dumfries Volunteers, and at the end of that August he had been elected to the Management Committee of the Corps. In the following month the death of little Elizabeth left him stunned - he had even been prevented from attending her funeral, which took place at Mauchline, due to his own ill-health. He informed Maria Riddell that his "domestic misfortune" had put all thought of his literary business out of his head.

His correspondence and his songwriting began to fall off in its output - he wrote to Mrs Dunlop, enclosing a copy of his song for the Volunteers, and wondered why she had not written to him, putting it down to the fact that, "in the hurry of momentous matters, I suppose such a trifling circumstance had escaped your recollection." Her recollections were obviously still centred on his letter expressing approval that, " a perjured Blockhead and unprincipled Prostitute" had perished by the blade of the guillotine. By the end of the year he was compelled to ask Excise Collector John Mitchell for the advance of one guinea, against his coming salary:

> Fu' fain I, modestly, would hint it,   (anxiously would)
> That ONE POUND, ONE, I sairly want it;   (sorely)
> If wi' the hizzie down ye sent it,   (hussy)
>   It would be kind;
> And while my heart wi' life-blood dunted, (throbbed)
>   I'd bear't in mind.

To this short verse epistle of three stanzas, to Mitchell, he added a postscript, informing the Collector of the concern for his health, and that a close brush with death had only just been avoided:

> Ye've heard this while now I've been licket,   (laid-low)
> And by fell Death 'maist nearly nicket;   (taken)
> Grim loon! he gat me by the fecket,   (shirt)
>   And sair he sheuk;   (sorely shook)
> But by good luck, I lap a wicket,   ("escaped")
>   And turn'd a neuk.[17]   (corner)

Well within the year his "good luck" ran out, and the poor bard was to find himself with no further 'neuk' to turn!

CHAPTER SIXTEEN

He Who of Rankin Sang

He who of Rankin sang, lies stiff and dead,
And a green grassy hillock hides his head;
Alas! Alas! a devilish change indeed.

Lines to John Rankin

FAREWELL, thou fair day; thou green earth; and ye skies,
    Now gay with the broad setting sun!
Farewell, loves and friendships, ye dear tender ties!
    Our race of existence is run.
Thou grim king of terrors, thou life's gloomy foe,
    Go frighten the coward and slave!
Go teach them to tremble, fell tyrant! but know,
    No terrors hast thou to the Brave!

The Song of Death.

The final year of Robert Burns's short life, 1796, opened amidst growing rumblings of discontent throughout the land. The poet tried once more to mend his breach with elderly Mrs Dunlop, and he wrote to her on 31 January, a few days after his thirty-seventh birthday, concluding the letter with some grave tidings:

> I know not how you are in Ayr-shire, but here, we have actual famine, & that too in the midst of plenty.- Many days my family & hundreds of other families, are absolutely without one grain of meal; as money cannot purchase it.- How long the *Swinish Multitude* will be quiet, I cannot tell: they threaten daily.- [1]

The reference to the *Swinish Multitude* was a swipe at the crass arrogance of Edmund Burke who had coined the phrase as a description of the common people. Burke is probably now best remembered as the man whose flowery prose had condemned every aspect of the French Revolution, and thus paved the way for several thumping replies, Thomas Paine's *Rights of Man*, and, James Mackintosh's *Vindiciae Gallicae*, being the most popular ones to survive.

An extremely unpopular government had considered it necessary to introduce two new Bills - one, the Treason Bill, which extended the scope of this crime to include mere words, spoken or written; the second, the Seditious Meetings Bill, forbade all political meetings and gatherings. There was justified uproar from the camp of the Whigs, the small democratic group led by Charles J Fox. A poem appeared in the *Morning Chronicle* for 25 January 1796, entitled, *Birthday Ode for Mr Fox*. His birthday was actually on 24 January; that, however, being a Sunday, the tribute was printed the following day, which, as it so happended, was the birthday of a certain radical poet. The poem carried no author's identification, and Patrick Scott Hogg listed it in his book, *The Lost Poems*, within the section, *Category B*, thus indicating that it was *possibly* the work of Burns. His latest researches, however, have directed him to the controversial Roman Catholic cleric, Alexander Geddes, the renowned biblical scholar, as being the more likely author of the *Ode to Fox*. Geddes, incidentally, is referred to by Burns as, "the supposed author" of the Jacobite song, *Lewis Gordon*.[2]

There was certainly no doubt about the author of the verses. *The Dean of the Faculty*, a political satire which arose from the mean-spirited fashion in which the liberal Henry Erskine was removed with unseemly haste from his position as the Dean of the Faculty of Advocates, and replaced by the Tory, Robert Dundas, Lord Advocate, and a nephew of Scotland's despot, Henry Dundas. Erskine's tenure in the office had lasted for ten years, and would surely have continued had he not openly declared his opposition to the newly introduced Bills. At the annual election, for the position of Dean, held on 12 January, he was heavily defeated, mustering only 38 votes to the 123 secured by Dundas. Burns's pen dripped with venomous sarcasm as he lashed out in his ballad, concluding with:

> In your heretic sins may ye live and die,
>   Ye heretic Eight and thirty!
> But accept, ye Sublime Majority,
>   My congratulations hearty.-
> With your Honors and a certain King
>   In your servants this is striking-
> The more incapacity they bring,
>   The more they're to your liking.-[3]

In the following month Burns suffered another severe attack of the rheumatic pains which must, by now, have been causing him considerable distress. According to Dr Currie this had either been brought-on, or at the very least, aggravated by a visit to a local tavern which resulted in him returning home in the early hours of a numbing cold morning, quite intoxicated. Not content to leave it at this, others sought to add the gory details that Burns had actually fallen down drunk, and slept off the effects of the alcohol, lying in the snow. James Mackay took the trouble to check-out the weather details of the time - there was no snow! In the year 1854, Thomas Thornburn of Ryedale, at the behest of Robert Chambers, attempted a thorough investigation into this alleged incident, and concluded that Burns had fallen asleep in the tavern, overcome by the illness he was suffering, and the effects of his medicine, rather than a binge of alcohol. Local tradition and ensuing gossip, rather than hard facts, are all that can now be related concerning this matter.

On the 24 February Burns wrote to James Johnson explaining that his long silence and lack of new songs had to do with the state of his health. The fact that the Excise paid his full salary for the period up to 3 March indicates that he probably was able to fulfil his employment commitments, or at least sufficiently so, to prevent them docking his wages. His next payment, in the six-week cycle, was due on 14 April, and, according to James Mackay's researches, this was reduced by half to the sum of £3. His salary again rose to £6 for the period ending 2 June, but fell to £2 on the last payment made to him by the Excise, on 14 July 1796. As Dr Mackay correctly states, this makes complete nonsense of the much peddled praise of the Excise Board by previous writers, from Currie onwards, who were under the illusion that Burns had continued to receive his full emoluments. Currie had, in fact, emphatically stated that the poet had received his full salary due to the kindness of Adam Stobbie, a young probationer in the Excise, who performed the duties of office without fee or reward. Burns related the situation to Alexander Cunningham, his friend in Edinburgh, thus:

> You actually would not know me if you saw me.- Pale, emaciated, & so feeble as occasionally to need help from my chair - my spirits fled! fled! - but I can no more on the subject - only the Medical folks tell me that my last & only chance is bathing & country quarters & riding.- The deuce of the matter is this; when an Excise-man is off duty, his salary is reduced to £35 instead

of £50.- What way, in the name of thrift, shall I maintain myself & keep a horse in Country-quarters - with a wife and five children at home, on £35? [4]

In the same letter Burns informed his friend that, the child which would be born within a week or two, if a boy, would be named Alexander Cunningham Burns in his honour - however, as it turned out, Jean Armour decided to name the little fellow, born on the day of his father's funeral, Maxwell - after his friend the doctor.

Why on earth the poor broken spirit of Robert Burns, in such a state of ill-health, could be directed to take a course of vigorous horse-riding, and bathe in the sea-water at Brow Well, now seems beyond the bounds of medical sanity, yet, he had somehow made the effort to leave his home at the end of June, and make his way to the bleak hole of isolation on the Solway coast. Catherine Carswell has given the following description of his quarters:

> Because it had a spring of mild chalybeate-water, which was contained in a red stone tank the size of a kitchen table, the place was dignified by the name of a spa. It was the Brow Well, no less. But provision for a sick man there was none. It was a mean, dilapidated, dismal little clachan, consisting of a dozen cottages and an inn that was no more than a cottage itself.[5]

Maria Riddell, who was also having trouble with her health at this time, had taken a break in the same area, closeby the village of Ruthwell; on 5 July she sent her carriage for the poet, inviting him to dine with her. Burns greeted her with the remark: "Well, Madam, and what are your commands for the next world?" - Maria brushed this aside with an exchange that, she was quite sure he would survive long enough to write her epitaph. As Catherine Carswell wrote: "Considering that he had already done so, and in the cruellest manner, it was a shrewd stroke."

They discussed his affairs, and Burns confided his concern to her that, pressing commitments and his declining health, had robbed him of the time which would have been necessary to put all his literary papers into a semblance of order. He was troubled that material was already being peddled around with his name attached to it, described by him as trash that he had neither written nor even seen. He had notified George Thomson that the copyright of the songs he had supplied for their project, was now effectively given over to the music publisher. Above all, he was depressed about the poverty which he now foresaw falling upon his wife and family.

On the 12 July Robert Burns dispatched two letters on what he clearly regarded as a matter of the utmost urgency. One was directed to his cousin, James Burness, in Montrose. The other, in similar appeal, was sent to George Thomson - Catherine Carswell has, arguably, described this matter better than other biographers:

> Two days later - when he was feeling somewhat better and believed himself to be benefiting by the treatment - the post brought a communication which came down like a hammerblow to his labouring heart. The tailor from whom he had bought his Volunteer uniform early in the preceding year was dissolving a partnership, and an attorney named Penn had been instructed in the usual way to collect outstanding debts. The letter was Penn's formal demand for £7:4s!
> To any man hard pressed for money, such a common form request would have been annoying. To Robert, in his morbid and critical condition and with his lifelong horror of debt, it was murderous. From the moment of its arrival it was never out of his thoughts. £7:4s! - a third of his annual salary as a sick man! And if he failed to pay, a debtor's prison! Thus he conceived it - 'the horrors of a jail.' [6]

His request for money to Burness and Thomson in order to cover the demand was met with an immediate and favourable response. His cousin sent him a draft for £10, the music publisher sent £5, which, incidentally, he himself had to borrow.

The letter to Thomson contained the very last song that Robert Burns ever composed, *Fairest Maid on Devon Banks,* which harked back to the period of his courtship with Peggy Chalmers at Harvieston on the banks of that river: thus the distinguished career of Britain's greatest songwriter concluded with the stanza:

> Then come, thou fairest of the fair,
> Those wonted smiles O let me share;
> And by thy beauteous self I swear,

Since these sentiments were directed to a heroine of former days, and written by the dying poet at the very time when his own wife was in the final stages of pregnancy, some writers appear to have found it an embarrassing situation. Allan Cunningham thought it safer that the Platonic Charlotte Hamilton, rather than the real love of Peggy Chalmers, inspired the final Muse. Another diversion is to lay claim that it was not the last song of Burns at all. James Mackay, and several others insist, against all the evidence that, *O, Wert Thou in the Cauld Blast,* concluded his career. He had composed this out of compliment to the young woman, Jessie Lewars, who nursed him, whilst attending to Jean and their young family, during his final days. Jessie informed Robert Chambers that Burns had called at her house one morning and asked her to play the piano. When she played the air, *Lenox Love to Blantyre,* Burns wrote the lyrics of his plaintive song. This must have been prior to his Brow Well visit; on his return from the spa Burns was completely bedridden, quite incapable of wandering from his house, to call upon Jessie.[8]

When the tides at the Brow Well were no longer suitable for bathing Burns decided it was time to go back home. In a letter to John Clark of Locharwoods written on 16 July, the poet sought permission to borrow his gig for the journey, which he made two days later. On arriving, in quite a shocking state of health, he wrote to James Armour, beseeching him to send Jean's mother down to Dumfries with all due haste; he informed his father-in-law that his strength had now gone, - his "disorder will prove fatal" to him. Three days later, on 21 July 1796, this statement sadly came true, and in the early hours of the morning Robert Burns died. Contradictions exist concerning his last words: some sources claim that he cried out in despair: "Syme, McMurdo, Maxwell, will none of you relieve me?" Robert jnr., who, with the other youngsters had been escorted into the room to take their farewell of him, maintained that, at the end, his father had cursed: "That damned rascal Matthew Penn" - the bill for his Volunteer's uniform thus being uppermost in his mind, even as he expired from the world.

The cause of his death, examined by modern medical research from the known facts such as they are, suggests that some form of heart disease, perhaps endocarditis, was to blame. Sir James Crichton-Browne, writing in

The Glasgow Herald in 1925, and published in the following year as a chapbook, came to this conclusion. A few years later, unaware of Crichton-Browne's writing, a Dr Anderson of Toronto, in a paper published in 1928, arrived at a very similar answer. Richard Fowler, however, has made some very valid points of criticism regarding Crichton-Browne's findings. The arguments which arise over the cause of the poet's death, somehow persist in examining what effect drink played in the issue. Crichton-Browne firmly believed that alcohol had no part in the origination of the illness that resulted in Burns's death, though he conceded that it may have hastened its progress. It was Fowler's view that Sir James was a specialist in mental health, who had but limited experience in clinical medicine. The fact that the pronouncement on the cause of Burns's death had been made by such an eminent man was sufficient, Fowler maintained, to sway many later scholars to accepting it as gospel truth, when doubts ought to have existed.[9] Richard Fowler, in turn, was unaware of the essay written by W W Buchanan and W F Kean, *Robert Burns's Illness Revisited,* (1982) which was published in the *Scottish Medical Journal.* They admitted it was now almost impossible to determine an accurate diagnosis after such a lapse of time; however, they gave some assurance that it was most unlikely that Burns had died of chronic alcoholism, venereal disease, or the result of extreme poverty or overwork, as suggested by some of those who had written about him. Buchanan and Kean have probably taken this matter as far along the way as it is going to go; their thesis is likely to remain as the authoritive voice on the morbid subject of the poet's terminal decline.[10]

The funeral of Robert Burns took place on Monday 26 July 1796 - his corpse, according to local tradition - was dressed in his Volunteer's uniform, and a twenty-strong party, formed by his compatriots of this body, performed the military duty at the graveside, though he had expressly forbidden that such action should take place. They had marched at the front, arms reversed, in the actual procession to St. Michael's churchyard, with the military band of the Cinque Ports Cavalry playing the *Dead March in Saul* - music which Burns surely would not have approved of at all. This cavalry was commanded by one, Robert Banks Jenkinson, later to serve the nation as Prime Minister, Lord Liverpool, one of the worst ever to hold the highest office of state. He had refused to shake the hand of Robert Burns whilst life still existed in the poet - and that was Jenkinson's crass misfortune. How fitting that Catherine Carswell should brand him "the celebrated nonentity", even if she did get his first name wrong! [11]

Among the poet's papers there was found a short epitaph which he had written on himself:

> He who of Rankin sang, lies stiff and dead,
> And a green grassy hillock hides his head;
> Alas! Alas! a devilish change indeed.[12]

Many years had passed since he had socialized with John Rankine of Adamhill farm back in Ayrshire. There is little doubt that he had simply dashed it off at this earlier period in his life, as a mock epitaph - he had a penchant for such pieces - though Dr Currie thought it may have been a deathbed composition, and this tradition has persisted in some quarters ever since. Another tradition has it that he told Jean Armour as he lay dying that, one hundred years hence, his name would resound far and wide to considerable peels of fame: "I'll be far mair thought of then" he allegedly murmured. It so happened that on the centenary of his death, in 1896, crowds such as never before seen in the area, descended on Dumfries, to commemorate the event. The Earl of Rosebery, the principal speaker, arose to ask: "Why have we gathered here in such a massive throng to honour the name of this man Robert Burns?" - and his lordship had a ready-made answer to his own question: "Because there has never been anybody quite like him!"

HE WHO OF RANKIN SANG

Source Notes

Chapter One: *No Distant Pretensions.*

1   *Kinsley, No. 140.* "There was a lad was born in Kyle". Lines 9-12 quoted.

2   See, *Burns - A Biography of Robert Burns:* by, James Mackay. Mainstream Publishing Company (Edinburgh) Ltd. (1992). In paperback by, Headline Book Publishing PLC, London. (1993). p. 19. For details of Burns's ancestry see, Chambers-Wallace (revised edition 1937) Vol. I, pp. 450-455.

3   *Letter No. 377.* (To Lady Winifred Maxwell Constable, 16 December, 1789. This letter passed from Sir Walter Scott to John G. Lockhart, his son-in-law, and biographer of both Scott and Burns. Scott commented: "to that singular old curmudgeon....you will see he plays high Jacobite, and on that account it is curious; though I fancy that his Jacobitism, like my own, belonged to the fancy rather than the reason." The original MS is in the Esty collection. Scott received his copy of the letter from Charles Kirkpatrick Sharpe on 20 July, 1828. This copy is now in the Laing collection).

4   Chambers-Wallace, Vol. I, p. 453.

5   *Robert Burns and the 18th-century Revival in Scottish Vernacular Poetry.* by, L M Angus Butterworth. Aberdeen University Press (1969). p 72.

6   *Kinsley No. 512.* Quoted in full.

Chapter Two: *By The Waters of Doon.*

1   *Robert Burns:* by Richard Hindle Fowler. Routledge London 1988. p. 123.

2   Letter from John Murdoch to Joseph Cooper Walker of Dublin. Murdoch's letter was later reproduced in James Currie's, *Complete Works of Robert Burns* (1800).

3   *Letter No. 125.* (Burns's Autobiography - i.e. the famous letter to Dr John Moore, dated, 2 August, 1787).

4   *Ibid.* It should be noted that Gilbert Burns maintained that Robert had not read *The Life of Wallace,* until several years afterwards, when he borrowed a copy from a local blacksmith.

5   Chambers-Wallace, Vol. I, p. 109

6   Letter form Gilbert Burns to Mrs Dunlop. It is now generally referred to as, *Gilbert's Narrative.*

Chapter Three: *The Sin of Rhyme.*

1 *Letter No. 125. (Autobiography).*
2 *Kinsley. No. 147B.* "I mind it weel in early date". Lines 29-34 quoted.
3 *The Tinder Heart:* by Hugh Douglas. Alan Sutton Publishing Limited (1996) p. 35. An extract of the letter to *The Scotsman* is given in James Mackay's biography of Burns, p. 51. Although Hugh Douglas says that: "James Mackay has unravelled the mystery of Handsome Nell's identity", this is far from being a proven case. Douglas himself, for instance, still names Nell Kilpatrick as the first of Burns's heroines, as late as p. 269 in, *The Tinder Heart.*
4 See, essay by Emily Lyle, *Love and Liberty: Robert Burns, A Bicentenary Celebration* ed. Kenneth Simpson. East Linton (1997) pp. 334-340.
5 This quotation was taken by Burns from John Milton's *Paradise Lost,* Bk. IV, line 269.
6 This particular phrase does not appear in certain copies of Burns's autobiography. It is found in the edition of Dr Currie, who, it was assumed by De Lancey Ferguson, worked from the poet's original draft, rather than the copy received by Moore.
7 *Kinsley, No. 2.* Lines 1-8 quoted.
8 Chambers-Wallace Vol I, p. 100n. The catalogue of Burns MSS compiled by Edward Clements Bigmore, sold at Leicester Sq., London, in May 1861, gives this verse and states that: "The name in the last line (Jeanie Armour) is given in shorthand." The poet's *Commonplace Book* also gives the verse with Armour's name in easily decoded cypher.
9 *Kinsley, No. 5.* Lines 1-8 quoted.
10 *Kinsley No. 71.* "Twas in that place o' Scotland's isle." Lines 93-100 quoted.

Chapter Four: *The Nature of the Bargain.*

1 See article, *To Inspire Such Passion,* by, Lesley Duncan, *The Herald,* 14 January, 1997.
2 Letter from David Sillar to Robert Aiken, in Morison's edition of Burns. Sillar's description of the poet is given in Chambers-Wallace, Vol. I, pp 68-69.
3 *Kinsley, No. 41.* "If ye gae up to yon hill-tap". Lines 17-24 quoted.
4 *Ibid., No. 40* "In Tarbolton ye ken....". Lines 25-28, and 33-40 quoted.
5 *Ibid., No. 6.* "Tibby I hae seen the day". Lines 5-8 quoted.

Chapter Five: *Montgomerie's Peggy.*

1 James Mackay (1992) p. 90.
2 *Reliques of Robert Burns:* Collected and published by, Robert H Cromek, Cadell and Davies, London 1808. pp. 442-4.
3 *Kinsley, No. 215.* "An I'll kiss thee yet, yet". Lines 5-8 quoted. (Cromek p. 441).
4 Cromek, *op. cit.* pp. 349-351.
5 James Mackay (1992) p. 86. See also n.45, p. 698.
6 *Kinsley, No. 11.* "On Cessnock banks a lassie dwells". Lines 49-52 quoted.
7 *Letter No. 9,* conjectured date 1781.
8 *Letter No. 3,* dated 12 June 1781.
9 Chambers-Wallace Vol I, p. 96.
10 *Popular Edition of Burns' Complete Works:* ed. William Scott Douglas, p. XXXVI.
11 James Mackay (1992) pp. 87-90.
12 James Mackay pp. 104-5, also, *Dirt & Deity, A Life of Robert Burns,* by Ian McIntyre. HarperCollins Publishers, 1995. pp. 37-8.

Chapter Six: *The Poor Man's Dearest Friend.*

1 Richard Fowler (1988) p. 130.
2 *Letter No. 16,* dated 17 Feb., 1784.
3 *Kinsley No. 35.* "O ye whose cheek the tear of pity stains". Lines 5-8 quoted.
4 *Ibid. No. 21.* "My father was a farmer....". Lines 1-4, and 29-36 quoted.
5 Richard Fowler (1988) has given a detailed account of John Locke's philosophy, and the effect that it had on Robert Burns - see, pp. 47-58.
6 *Kinsley No. 64.* "When chill November's Surly blast". Lines 81-88 quoted.
7 *Life of Robert Burns:* by, John G Lockhart. J M Dent & Sons Ltd., 1907 (reprinted 1959). p. 52.
8 Scott Douglas, *op. cit.* Vol I, p. 65.
9 *Kinsley, No. 72.* "My lov'd, my honor'd, much respected friend". Lines 172-189 quoted.

Chapter Seven: *Rob Mossgiel.*

1   *Kinsley, No. 51.* "While winds frae off Ben-Lomond blow". 57-70 quoted.

2   *The Russet Coat:* by, Christina Keith. Robert Hale Ltd., 1956. p. 56. Presumably she means that the only decent song written for Jean Armour was *Of A' the Airts* - fourteen songs have been attributed to Armour in J. C. Dick's *Songs of Robert Burns.* (1903).

3   *The Poetry of Robert Burns:* ed. W E Henley and T F Henderson. Caxton Publishing Company Limited, London. 1896. Vol. I, p. 369.

4   *Kinsley, No. 42.* quoted in full.

5   The poem *Libel Summons* is given in Kinsley's edition as No. 109.

6   Cromek, *op. cit.,* p. 340.

7   *The Story of Robert Burns:* by, John S Clarke. Scottish Workers Press, Glasgow. *c.* 1922. p. 7.

8   The legality of the Burns-Armour irregular marriage is considered in Chambers-Wallace, Vol. I, p 313n. This has been repeated in James Mackay's biography of the poet, pp. 181-2. Gilbert Burns stated that, Robert and Jean had agreed that they should make a legal acknowledgement of their marriage. Gilbert added that the Armours insisted that the written papers respecting the marriage should be cancelled, thus rendering the union void. All that can be said with certainty is that Robert regarded his written document as a legally binding marriage; whether, or not, he took advice on this from one of the lawyers with whom he was friendly, is not known.

9   *Some Aspects of Robert Burns.* by, Robert Louis Stevenson (Scottish Classic Reprints, Sea-Green Ribbon Publications, Fareham 1996) p. 6.

10   *Letter No. 25,* dated 15 April, 1786.

11   *Letter No. 29,* conjectured date, April 1786.

12   *Kinsley, No. 79.* "Dear Smith, the sleest, pawkie thief". Lines 31-54 quoted.

13   *Letter No. 36,* dated 30 July, 1786.

14   *Kinsley, No. 104.* "Is there a whim-inspir'd fool". Lines 19-30 quoted.

Chapter Eight: *Farewell To Ayrshire.*

1   *Kinsley, No. 9.* Lines 1-8 quoted.

2   James Mackay (1992) pp. 72, 89-90, 154, and 201. On p.149 Mackay states that: "The tradition that Robert was sweet on her (Elizabeth Miller) was entirely based on the supposition that she was the heroine of 'From Thee, Eliza, I must go', composed at least three years before he met her." Mackay, however, appears to contradict himself elsewhere by suggesting that there is "strong evidence" that Burns did court Elizabeth Miller. See, pp. 156 and 298.

3   Ian McIntyre (1990) p. 93.

4   *The Life of Robert Burns:* by, Catherine Carswell (Canongate Classics 30) p. 175. First published, 1930, by Wm. Collins & Sons. Reprinted by Canongate Publishing Limited, Edinburgh (1990).

5   *The Life of Robert Burns.* by, Franklyn Bliss Snyder. The Macmillan Company, New York, 1932 p. 144.

6   James Mackay (1992) pp. 226-7.

7   *Kinsley, No. 130.* "When biting Boreas fell and doure". Lines 44-58 quoted. It has only recently come to light that an abridged version of this poem was published in *The Gentleman's Magazine,* August 1794, under the title, *Humanity: An Ode.* See article, *Discovery of a Lost World ,* by, Patrick Scott Hogg, *The Herald,* 24, Jan., 1998.

8   See, Henley & Henderson, Vol. II, p. 361. The term 'dulcinea' simply means lady-love; Burns may have obtained it from the works of Laurence Sterne: "I must ever have some Dulcinea in my head - it harmonises the soul."

9   *Letter No. 58,* dated 20 Nov., 1786.

Chapter Nine: *Scotia's Darling Seat.*

1   *Robert Burns as a Freemason:* by, William Harvey. T M Sparks & Son, Dundee, 1944. Murray Lyon, however, in the same publication, is quoted as stating that Burns was elected to the office of Poet-Laureate of the Lodge, see, pp. 33-4.

2   *Robert Burns: The Man & The Poet,* by, Robert Fitzhugh, Houghton Mifflin company, Boston 1970. p. 132.

3   *Ibid.* p.130.

4   *Kinsley, No. 136.* "Fair fa' your honest, sonsie face". Lines 43-48 quoted.

5   *Letter No. 324,* dated, 25 March 1789. According to Catherine

Carswell, the total sum given over to Gilbert was £300. See,
Carswell, (reprint 1990) p. 400.

6   *Kinsley, No. 154.* "Auld chuckie Reekie's sair distress". Lines 7-12;
    and, 25-36 quoted.
7   *Ibid. No. 276.* "Cease, ye prudes...." Quoted in full.
8   *Ibid. No. 335,* "Late crippled of an arm...." Additional lines 13-20
    quoted. Burns had intended to write a lengthy poem titled, *The Poet's
    Progress,* but made no headway on it. The fragment to Smellie was
    thus incorporated into the poem, *To Robert Graham.* Burns's letters
    to Smellie were destroyed. Robert Kerr, Smellie's biographer (1811)
    claimed that they were "totally unfit for publication" due to the fact
    that they reflected very badly on certain people.
9   *Ibid., No. 159.* Epigram, Lines 1-4 quoted.
10 *The Letters of Robert Burns:* edited by, John De Lancey Ferguson,
    Vol. I, p. 116.
11 *Kinsley, No. 166.* "Here Stewarts once in triumph reigned". Lines 7-
    10 quoted.
12 *Letter No. 145,* dated, 20 October 1787.

Chapter Ten: *Beneath The Ochill Hills*

1   *Letter No. 76.* Addressed to My Dear Countrywoman, undated, taken
    from a draft copy found by Dr Currie among Burns's papers. The
    majority of Burns scholars have identified Peggy Chalmers as the
    recipient. Others, however, have suggested that it was Christina
    Lawrie. It should be noted that she was engaged to a Glasgow
    bookseller, Alexander Wilson, during this period, and married him on
    19 April 1787. It is quite inconceivable that Burns would have
    addressed her in such language of love, being aware of her personal
    circumstances. Therefore, the letter was almost certainly written with
    Peggy Chalmers in mind, and possibly sent to her. The internal
    evidence suggests a date in the early part of 1787.
2   *Kinsley, No. 182.* "Where braving angry Winter's Storms". Lines 9-
    16 quoted.
3   *Letter No. 272,* dated 16 Sept. 1788.
4   *The Wonder of all the Gay World:* by James Barke, p. 7 - see also, the
    chapter titled, *Corporal Trim's Hat,* pp. 154-9.
5   See, article, *The Letters of "Clarinda" to "Sylvander",* by James C
    Ewing, *Burns Chronicle* 1934, pp. 72-77.

6   *Letter No. 199,* dated 13 Feb., 1788.

7   *Burns Chronicle, op. cit.,* 1934. p. 73.

8   See, *Letters,* Ferguson, Vol. II, p. 358-9.

9   *Kinsley No. 337.* "Ae fond kiss...". Lines 21-24 quoted.

10   *Letter No. 210,* dated 23 Feb., 1788.

11   Richard Fowler (1988) p. 189.

12   *Kinsley, No. 193,* quoted in full.

Chapter Eleven: *Land of God's Riddings.*

1   In his biography of Jean Armour, Peter Westwood gives a specific date of 2 May, 1788, for the marriage ceremony, and adds that it took place in Gavin Hamilton's house, or business chambers. However, he gives no authority for this; the date in May is at variance with Burns's letter to James Smith. See, *Jean Armour, Mrs Robert Burns:* by, Peter J Westwood. Creedon Publications, Dumfries. 1996. p.39.

2   Robert Louis Stevenson (reprint 1996) pp. 12-13.

3   Peter J Westwood. *op. cit.,* pp. 114-15.

4   *Kinsley, No. 222.* "In this strange land...". Lines 7-18 quoted.

5   *Letter No. 325,* dated 2 April, 1789.

6   Ian McIntyre (1995) p. 241.

7   *Letter No. 507,* dated 16 Sept., 1792.

8   Richard Fowler (1988) p. 143. Concerning this incident, James Mackay is quite critical towards Burns in his biography, pp. 434-4; however, by p. 448, Mackay's attitude has softened quite considerably, even suggesting that Mitchell and Findlater may have ignited the idea of Smith's removal to Burns, which is ridiculous!

9   Richard Fowler, pp. 148-9.

10   See, article in *Weekend Guardian* 25-26 Jan., 1991, by Alistair Campsie. The same writer has woven this theory into his novel, *The Clarinda Conspiracy,* Mainstream Publishing Co. (Edinburgh) Ltd. 1989.

11   *Letter no. 373,* dated 9 Dec., 1789.

12   *Kinsley, No. 264.* Lines 1-5, and, 70-74 quoted. It should be noted that most editions give two postcript, or presentation stanzas, at the conclusion of this ballad.

13   *Letter No. 374,* dated 13 Dec., 1789.

14   See, James Mackay (1988) pp. 208-9, also p. 461.

15   *Letter No. 381,* dated 11 Jan., 1790. (date taken from cover).

Chapter Twelve: *The Banks of Nith*

1   *Kinsley, No. 269.* "There was five Carlins...". Lines 9-12 quoted.
2   *Ibid. No. 270.* "The Laddies by the banks of Nith". Lines 5-8 quoted.
3   Ian McIntyre pp. 293-6, who concludes by describing the incident as being, *ben trovato,* (characteristic, if not true). James Mackay, 499-502, described Robert's action as "somewhat eccentric and audaciously generous", perhaps implying that it did, in his opinion, actually occur.
4   Letter from Alexander Findlater to the Editor of Johnstone's *Edinburgh Magazine,* Feb., 1834.
5   *Letter No. 558,* dated 13 April, 1793.
6   See, article, *Poetry and Politics: Burns and Revolution:* by W J Murray. *Studies in the Eighteenth Century IV* (Australian National University Press, 1979). pp. 57-82. (Reprinted in *Burns Chronicle* 1990).
7   *Letter No. 497,* dated, Feb., 1792.
8   *Kinsley, No. 426,* "Praise woman still...". Lines 5-8 quoted.
9   *Highland Mary:* ed. John D Ross. Published by Alexander Gardner, Paisley. 1894. pp. 30-31.
10 Henley & Henderson. Vol. IV, p. 289.
11 John D Ross, who wrote: "There is only one redeeming feature about the Essay - and only one - it was not written by a Scotsman. Thank Heaven for that!" *(Henley and Burns,* Stirling, 1901).
12 See article, *New Versions of Robert Burns's Great Song:* by, Patrick Scott Hogg, for some interesting comments on this song: *Burns Chronicle,* 1997, pp. 120-123.
13 The reference here is to the first set of the song, given by Kinsley as No. 185. A second set is given as No. 456, *Ca' the yowes to the knowes* (B), and is Burns's composition, the chorus apart. Jean Lorimer may well have been the inspiration of the second set.
14 See chapbook, *Auld Lang Syne:* by, G Ross Roy. The Black Pennell Press, Greenock. 1984.

Chapter Thirteen: *Heresies In Church and State.*

1   *Letter No. 544,* conjectured date, March 1793.
2   *Robert Burns: The Lost Poems:* by, Patrick Scott Hogg. Clydeside Press, Glasgow, 1997. p. 78-91.

3   *Muir of Huntershill:* by, Christina Bewley. Oxford University Press, 1981. p. 67.

4   *Scotland and the French Revolution:* by, Henry W. Meikle. (James Maclehose and Sons, Edinburgh 1912. Reprinted Augustus M Kelley, Publishers, New York, 1969), p. 135.

5   *Kinsley No. 425.* "Scots, wha hae wi' Wallace bled". Lines 17-24 quoted.

6   *Robert Burns: The Lost Poems. op. cit.,* pp. 105-122.

7   *Here and There in Two Hemispheres:* by, James D. Law. Home Publishing Company, Lancaster, Philadelphia. U.S.A., 1903. p. 461.

8   *Kinsley No. 401.* Lines 1-5 quoted. (Slight misspelling of names in Burns's text).

9   Not given in Kinsley's edition. See, Henley & Henderson, Vol. II p. 255. See also notes on this piece in same Vol, p. 442.

10   Patrick Miller told Sir Walter Scott that James Perry had offered Burns 5gns. per week. (See Chambers-Wallace Vol. IV, p. 116 n.). This is repeated by Catherine Carswell, see, p. 361 of her *Burns.* James Mackay, however, states that Perry's offer was one guinea per week. (See, Mackay, p. 580). There may have been two separate proposals put to Burns, the higher offer being conditional on him moving to London and accepting full-time staff employment with the 'paper.

11   Patrick Scott Hogg, writing in *The Herald,* 24 Jan., 1998, has stated that several leading Burns scholars have now accepted some of the discovered poems as very likely the work of Burns. See article, *Discovery of a Lost World.*

12   *Letter No. 604,* dated Dec., 1793 - but revised in 2nd Edition to, No. 499A, conjectured date, Feb., 1792.

13   Catherine Carswell (Reprint 1990) p. 355.

14   *Ibid.* pp. 355-6.

Chapter Fourteen: *The Lintwhite Locks of Chloris*

1   *Letter No. 632,* dated, July 1794.

2   *Kinsley, No. 466.* "Lassie wi' the lintwhite locks". Lines 17-20 quoted.

3   James Mackay (1992)) p. 577.

4   *Letter No. 689,* dated, Feb., 1796.

5   Chloris, in Greek, means verdant, green.

6   Chambers-Wallace Vol. IV, p. 158.

7   *Letter No. 687,* dated, Jan, 1796.

8   *Letter No. 650,* conjectured date, Jan., 1795.
9   Henley & Henderson. Vol. III, pp. 489-490.
10   *Op. cit., Poetry and Politics:* by, W J Murray pp. 79-80.
11   *Ibid.* p. 80.

Chapter Fifteen: *Bold John Barleycorn*

1   *Kinsley, No. 77.* "Let other poets raise a fracas". Lines 7-12 quoted.
2   *Ibid. No. 81.* "Ye Irish Lords, ye knights an' squires". Lines 181-186 quoted.
3   James Mackay (1992) p. 674. Alan Bold was, however, making a point that Burns worked in creative bursts, Mossgiel being the prime example; Bold was surely not implying that Burns indulged in an alcoholic bout concurrently.
4   *Kinsley, No. 272.* "I sing of a Whistle, a Whistle of worth". Lines 41-44 quoted.
5   Sir Walter Scott to John G. Lockhart, 11 March, 1828. See, Robert Fitzhugh (1970) p. 11. See also, James Mackay (1992) p. 664. The opinion regarding Burns's relationship with Miller not being particularly good is hardly justified by Burns's letter of March 1793, in which he offers Miller a copy of his poems as: "A mark of my gratitude to you, as a Gentleman to whose goodness I have been much indebted; of my respect for you, as a Patriot who...stands forth the champion of the liberties of my Country; & of my veneration for you, as a Man whose benevolence of heart does honor to Human-nature."
6   For details of the case against Lewars see, *William Maxwell to Robert Burns:* by, Robert D Thornton. John Donald Publishers Ltd., Edingburgh, 1979. pp. 165-9. It is interesting to note that, Burns's neighbour, the 'smith George Haugh, was a witness to the charges. Prof. Thornton has adequately examined the facts which allowed, "Lewars to get off Scot-free", and Burns to "keep his name out of the proceedings except for Lewars' identification of him as the other person."
7   Richard Fowler (1988) pp. 239-242.
8   James Mackay (1992) p. 679.
9   *Ibid* p. 447, also at p. 475. Brydges, at this specific time, was involved in a protracted legal wrangle to obtain the barony of Chandos. The initial hearing took place in the House of Lords in June 1790, with

twenty-six further hearings thereafter following. He could not have spared the time to make the long journey from London to Ellisland. Robert Chambers, Scott Douglas, Dr Robert Carruthers, and James C Ewing have all pointed out that Brydges indulged in a fanciful, *i.e.* imaginary visit.

10 The song notes were given by Burns in Glenriddel's interleaved copy of James Johnson's *Scots Musical Museum* (see, Chambers-Wallace Vol. IV, pp. 405-6). The first and last, of four stanzas, are quoted, *Kinsley No. 268.*

11 Henley & Henderson Vol. III, 359-360.

12 Ian McIntyre (1995) p. 120.

13 *Kinsley, No. 77.* Introductory lines to *Scotch Drink.*

14 For details of Patrick Heron's political career see, *The House of Commons 1790-1820,* by, R. G. Thorne, (History of Parliament Trust; Secker & Warburg: 1986).

15 *Kinsley No. 491.* "Wham will we send to London town" Lines 53-56 quoted.

16 *Letter No. 675.* (2nd Edition 673A.) conjectured date, Summer 1795.

17 *Kinsley No. 514.* "Friend o' the Poet, tried and leal". Lines 7-12 and 19-24 quoted.

Chapter Sixteen: *He Who of Rankin Sang*

1 *Letter No. 688,* dated 31 Jan., 1796. Burns's comment that, "the people threaten daily", proved true. There were serious food riots in Dumfries during March. See, *Apostle to Burns: The Diaries of William Grieson,* ed. by, John Davies. (William Blackwood, Edinburgh, 1981). pp. 55-7, entries for Sat., 12 - Tues., 15 March 1796.

2 *Op. cit, Discovery of a Lost World,* by Patrick Scott Hogg. Burns, in the song notes compiled for Robert Riddell in the interleaved copy of the *Scots Musical Museum* wrote: "The supposed author of the song was a Mr Geddes, priest, at Shenval in the Ainzie." (Enzie of Banffshire). Geddes, from the early 1780's, until his death in 1802, resided in London, where he had, in effect, abandoned the priesthood.

3 *Kinsley No. 515.* "Dire was the hate at old Harlaw". Lines 33-40 quoted.

4 *Letter No. 700.* dated 7 July, 1796.

5 Catherine Carswell (reprint 1990) pp. 375-6.

6 *Ibid,* pp. 378-9.

7 *Kinsley No. 525.* "Fairest maid on Devon banks." Lines 9-12 quoted.

8 Chambers-Wallace, Vol. IV, p. 267. The rather quaint title of the air, *Lenox love to Blantyre,* was taken from an estate of that name, owned by the fifth Lord Blantyre. His aunt, the Duchess of Richmond and Lenox, who died in 1702, had willed him the bulk of her considerable wealth, with instructions to purchase an estate in East Lothian and name it after her. According to Chambers-Wallace, the tune played by Jessie Lewars was, *The Wren's Nest,* SMM No. 406 - most sources, however, conclude that it was *The Wren (Lenox love to Blantyre)* SMM No. 483, which provided the tune for the song.

9 Richard Fowler (1988) pp. 212-216.

10 The essay by Drs Buchanan and Kean was reprinted in a separate pamphlet in 1982, and was, at that time, available from these doctors at, McMaster University, Hamilton, Ontario, Canada.

11 Catherine Carswell (reprint 1990) p. 383. Mrs Carswell names, Hon. Charles Jenkinson; he was the father of "the celebrated nonentity", who became Lord Liverpool the premier.

12 *Kinsley No. 50.* quoted in full. Kinsley gives John Rankin in cypher. In Poem No. 48, the farmer of Adamhill has his surname spelt Ranken, and this, presumably, was how Burns spelt it. Most biographers, and editors of Burns's works, give the name as Rankine. Kinsley, in Poem No. 47, although again giving the surname in cypher, indicates a seven letter name, (Rankine in index of short titles) - as it was given by Dr Currie in 1800.

INDEX